Life-Giving Encouragement from
Ecclesiastes

30 Devotions and Insights from
Our Daily Bread

Our Daily Bread
Publishing.

Life-Giving Encouragement from Ecclesiastes: 30 Devotions and Insights from Our Daily Bread
© 2024 by Our Daily Bread Ministries

Some devotional readings collected in this book were previously published over a span of years in *Our Daily Bread* devotional booklets that are distributed around the world in more than fifty languages.

The Ecclesiastes outline on page 25 and other material as noted throughout are from David A. Dorsey, *The Literary Structure of the Old Testament: A Commentary on Genesis–Malachi* ("Table 20.7 The Book of Ecclesiastes," 198), Baker Academic, a division of Baker Publishing Group, 1999. Used by permission.

Interior design by Patti Brinks

ISBN: 978-1-64070-254-7

Library of Congress Cataloging-in-Publication Data Available

Printed in the United States of America
24 25 26 27 28 29 30 31 / 8 7 6 5 4 3 2 1

There is a time for everything, and a season for
every activity under the heavens.

Ecclesiastes 3:1

Introduction

Welcome to the timely, life-giving book of Ecclesiastes. During the next thirty days, be guided by trusted devotional authors from *Our Daily Bread* through this ancient book, unlocking its outstanding wisdom and contemporary guidance. Each day's devotion—along with the accompanying Bible text and study tools—will help you navigate life in an uncertain world.

More than most any other book of the Bible, Ecclesiastes gives you permission to ask questions about life's heartaches, limitations, and hard things. In the end, it may not answer all your *whys*—but instead reveals that a life of joy, meaning, and purpose is found through giving yourself to the mystery of the *Who*: in surrendering to the unsearchable wisdom of the One who holds the cosmos, every detail of your life, and all of your unknowns in His hands.

The Creator is completely trustworthy, totally sovereign, and infinitely merciful and compassionate.

In *Life-Giving Encouragement from Ecclesiastes*, you will discover the boundless joy, immeasurable satisfaction, and incomparable peace of living in trusting dependence on God, even when your journey is unexpected.

Anna Haggard
General Editor

Day 1

Ecclesiastes 1:1–11

[1] *The words of the Teacher, son of David, king in Jerusalem:*

[2] *"Meaningless! Meaningless!"*
says the Teacher.
"Utterly meaningless!
Everything is meaningless."

[3] *What do people gain from all their labors*
at which they toil under the sun?
[4] *Generations come and generations go,*
but the earth remains forever.
[5] *The sun rises and the sun sets,*
and hurries back to where it rises.
[6] *The wind blows to the south*
and turns to the north;
round and round it goes,
ever returning on its course.
[7] *All streams flow into the sea,*
yet the sea is never full.
To the place the streams come from,
there they return again.
[8] *All things are wearisome,*
more than one can say.
The eye never has enough of seeing,
nor the ear its fill of hearing.

⁹ *What has been will be again,*
   what has been done will be done again;
   there is nothing new under the sun.
¹⁰ *Is there anything of which one can say,*
   "Look! This is something new"?
It was here already, long ago;
   it was here before our time.
¹¹ *No one remembers the former generations,*
   and even those yet to come
will not be remembered
   by those who follow them.

Finding Meaning in the Mundane

Katara Patton

What do people gain from all their labors at
which they toil under the sun?

Ecclesiastes 1:3

After an exhausting day of working as a nurse—giving meds to the sick, charting vital signs, monitoring moods of patients, family members, and coworkers—my sister signed out of work. She had been working as a nurse for more than thirty years. Physically, she was tired. Emotionally, she was drained. She just wanted to get in her car and drive to the comfort of her home. But this day, someone stopped her before she could leave the hospital lobby. "You were my husband's nurse," the voice exclaimed as my sister reluctantly stopped to listen to a woman. "He died a while ago, but because of your kindness, I volunteer at this hospital. I want others to feel the same care I felt from you." After thanking the woman for her words, my sister's mood lifted. Her job often felt tedious and meaningless, but was it really?

While pondering the routines of life, the teacher in Ecclesiastes exclaims, "Meaningless! Meaningless!" (1:2). The teacher ponders what we gain from all of our work (v. 3). It can be tough to recognize our impact—or even the purpose of our work—when we're stuck in the daily routine. You do what you're conditioned to do, sometimes mindlessly plowing through life.

But even in the midst of mundane tasks, we can impact others, especially when we work to honor God (Colossians 3:23). Even during routine tasks, we can serve Him through our actions and attitudes.

> What tasks are you doing that feel mundane? Ask God how He sees your work or how you are serving Him through it.

Introducing Ecclesiastes

Ecclesiastes has been described as the Bible book for the post-modern world. The Teacher (likely King Solomon, see Ecclesiastes 1:1) approaches life with the cynicism of someone who has had it all and been left empty. As one commentator points out, "What place does this book have in the Bible? Many have asked this question in the light of its pessimism and humanistic sentiments. Primarily it acts as a foil or contrast to the other books. It is a brilliant, artful argument for the way one would look at life—*if* God did *not* play a direct, intervening role in life and *if* there were no life after death." [1]

As is typical with the Hebrew Bible, the book's name comes from the first key word or idea—the Preacher (v. 1). It is the Hebrew term for the one who leads the congregation (the Preacher, *Koheleth*, the Teacher), and its Greek equivalent is *ecclesiastes*.

word study

Meaningless

[*hebel*] (v. 2)

If we stopped at these eleven verses, we might well conclude all is lost. The Hebrew word for *meaningless*—*hebel*—is used five times in the Hebrew text of Ecclesiastes 1:2, an astonishing number because there are only eight different words in the entire verse! *Hebel* literally means "vapor" or "breath." Through this image, the Teacher describes things that—like a vapor—are hard to grasp, short-lived, or insubstantial.

Hebel is a guiding theme of Ecclesiastes. As used here, *hebel* is interpreted as "utterly meaningless" and conveys an overwhelming sense of hopelessness through its use of the superlative. Other versions render it as "completely meaningless," "futility of futilities," "absolute futility," and "vanity of vanities." According to the author, things couldn't be more meaningless. This is not quite the way we would expect a holy writing to begin, yet such raw honesty only enhances the value of Ecclesiastes for us.

Day 2

Ecclesiastes 1:12–15

¹² *I, the Teacher, was king over Israel in Jerusalem.* ¹³ *I applied my mind to study and to explore by wisdom all that is done under the heavens. What a heavy burden God has laid on mankind!* ¹⁴ *I have seen all the things that are done under the sun; all of them are meaningless, a chasing after the wind.*

¹⁵ *What is crooked cannot be straightened;*
what is lacking cannot be counted.

Beyond the Sun

Tim Gustafson

What a heavy burden God has laid on mankind!
Ecclesiastes 1:13

Philosopher and writer Albert Camus (1913–1960) was a complex man. He didn't believe in God, viewing life as accidental—meaningless. Yet while denying life's purpose, he astoundingly still risked his life on behalf of moral truth, opposing communistic regimes and the Nazis.

Another great thinker believed in God yet struggled with finding meaning. "The Teacher" (1:12) (likely King Solomon) possessed everything this world had to offer only to conclude that God has placed "a heavy burden" on his creatures (v. 13). "I have seen all the things that are done under the sun," the Teacher wrote; "all of them are meaningless, a chasing after the wind" (v. 14). He saw our situation as hopeless: "What is crooked cannot be straightened" (v. 15).

Eventually, the Teacher circled back to our "burden"—and found hope. He wrote, "I have seen the burden God has laid on the human race. He has made everything beautiful in its time. He has also set eternity in the human heart; yet no one can fathom what God has done from beginning to end" (3:10–11).

We seek fulfillment "under the sun," but God has placed in us a sense that there is much more. If we found complete fulfillment here, we wouldn't realize what we're missing. We wouldn't hunger for God.

We don't find our purpose under the sun, but beyond it.

> Identify several limitations that come from living "under the sun" (v. 14).

> Why can't we "fathom what God has done from beginning to end" (3:11)?

Under the Sun

The phrase "under the sun," which is repeated constantly in Ecclesiastes, is an idiom likely close in meaning to "on the earth." When reflecting on "all the things that are done under the sun" (1:14), the Teacher is referring not just to daytime activities, but to all human activities and experiences on our planet.

We still use similar language today. For example, we might say we tried "everything on earth" or "everything under the sun"—meaning we tried everything humanly possible.

Ecclesiastes uses the similar phrase "under the sun" so often because it gets at the core issue the Teacher wrestles with: whether human beings—who have little control over what happens on the earth and whose lives unavoidably end in death (2:15)—can still find hope and meaning (v. 17).

Unlocking the Meaning of Ecclesiastes

One of the secrets to understanding Ecclesiastes is through uncovering the phrase "under the sun" (see Under the Sun). Through it, the Teacher reveals our excruciating predicament: As humans, we know a big picture exists (3:11).[2] Because of our narrow vantage point "under the sun," however, we can't access it (3:10–11; 8:17). Life's meaning is obstructed by our narrow, temporary, under-the-sun perspective. Only the One above the sun—the omniscient, omnipresent, and omnipotent God—has the thirty-thousand-foot view (3:11).

Only He can see life's meaning within the scaffolding of eternity.

Though while "under the sun," we cannot grasp our full purpose, the Teacher says there is hope: we can entrust ourselves to the sovereign, limitless, and compassionate God (5:7; 12:13) who alone comprehends life's meaning, purpose, and significance "from beginning to end" (3:11).

Day 3

Ecclesiastes 1:16–18

¹⁶ *I said to myself, "Look, I have increased in wisdom more than anyone who has ruled over Jerusalem before me; I have experienced much of wisdom and knowledge."* ¹⁷ *Then I applied myself to the understanding of wisdom, and also of madness and folly, but I learned that this, too, is a chasing after the wind.*

¹⁸ *For with much wisdom comes much sorrow;*
the more knowledge, the more grief.

When Knowledge Hurts

Mike Wittmer

For with much wisdom comes much sorrow;
the more knowledge, the more grief.
Ecclesiastes 1:18

Zach Elder and his friends pulled up to shore after a twenty-five-day rafting trip through the Grand Canyon. The man who came to retrieve their rafts told them about the COVID-19 virus. They thought he was joking. But as they left the canyon their phones pinged with their parents' urgent messages. Zach and his friends were stunned. They wished they could return to the river and escape what they now knew.

In a fallen world, knowledge often brings pain. The wise Teacher of Ecclesiastes observed, "With much wisdom comes much sorrow; the more knowledge, the more grief" (1:18). Who hasn't envied a child's blissful ignorance? She doesn't yet know about racism, violence, and cancer. Weren't we happier before we grew up and discerned our own weaknesses and vices? Before we learned our family's secrets—why our uncle drinks heavily or what caused our parents' divorce?

The pain from knowledge can't be wished away. Once we know, it's no use pretending we don't. But there's a higher knowledge that empowers us to endure, even thrive. Jesus is the Word of God, the light that shines in our darkness (John 1:1–5). He "has become for us wisdom from God—that is, our righteousness, holiness and redemption" (1 Corinthians 1:30). Your pain is your reason to run to Jesus. He knows you and cares for you.

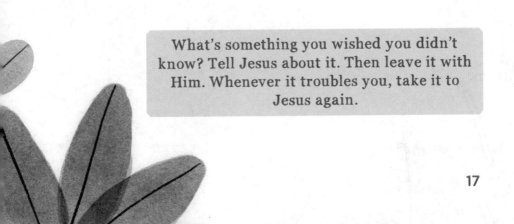

What's something you wished you didn't know? Tell Jesus about it. Then leave it with Him. Whenever it troubles you, take it to Jesus again.

word study

Wisdom

[*chokmah*] (v. 11)

In Scripture, *chokmah*—wisdom—can be understood as the art of living a good, rich life. Proverbs tells us that *chokmah* is a quality of God built into creation (3:19–20). Human flourishing requires awe and reverence for God (3:19) and humbly submitting to God's wisdom. In Proverbs, wisdom is described as a source of deep joy as well as protection (2:10–12).

In Ecclesiastes, the Teacher likewise understands wisdom as a gift of God (2:26) of great value (3:13–14; 7:11–12). But the Teacher was also deeply aware that in a world marred by injustice and death, wisdom is no panacea. It can actually increase pain at the world's brokenness (1:18), and it cannot protect the wise from death (2:14–15). Wisdom also can't provide people with control over their lives or full understanding—complete understanding remains always out of grasp, "a chasing after the wind" (1:14).

Prayer

Father in heaven, I long to know.
To know why.
To know how long.
To know toward what great end You direct my life.

But in my longing to know I so often fail to trust that You know.
You know my beginning and my end,
My failings and my faithfulness,
Even my moments of secret sorrow.

So teach me to trust my God-who-knows, and that I may join
Your Son and say,
"Let it be done as you wish."

In the name of the Son, who surrendered
to Your will,

Amen.

Day 4

Ecclesiastes 2:1–16

¹ I said to myself, "Come now, I will test you with pleasure to find out what is good." But that also proved to be meaningless. ² "Laughter," I said, "is madness. And what does pleasure accomplish?" ³ I tried cheering myself with wine, and embracing folly—my mind still guiding me with wisdom. I wanted to see what was good for people to do under the heavens during the few days of their lives.

⁴ I undertook great projects: I built houses for myself and planted vineyards. ⁵ I made gardens and parks and planted all kinds of fruit trees in them. ⁶ I made reservoirs to water groves of flourishing trees. ⁷ I bought male and female slaves and had other slaves who were born in my house. I also owned more herds and flocks than anyone in Jerusalem before me. ⁸ I amassed silver and gold for myself, and the treasure of kings and provinces. I acquired male and female singers, and a harem as well—the delights of a man's heart. ⁹ I became greater by far than anyone in Jerusalem before me. In all this my wisdom stayed with me.

¹⁰ I denied myself nothing my eyes desired;
    I refused my heart no pleasure.
My heart took delight in all my labor,
    and this was the reward for all my toil.

¹¹ *Yet when I surveyed all that my hands had done*
    and what I had toiled to achieve,
everything was meaningless, a chasing after the wind;
    nothing was gained under the sun.

¹² *Then I turned my thoughts to consider wisdom,*
    and also madness and folly.
What more can the king's successor do
    than what has already been done?
¹³ *I saw that wisdom is better than folly,*
    just as light is better than darkness.
¹⁴ *The wise have eyes in their heads,*
    while the fool walks in the darkness;
but I came to realize
    that the same fate overtakes them both.

¹⁵ *Then I said to myself,*

> *"The fate of the fool will overtake me also.*
>   *What then do I gain by being wise?"*
> *I said to myself,*
>   *"This too is meaningless."*
¹⁶ *For the wise, like the fool, will not be long remembered;*
    the days have already come when both have been
        forgotten.
Like the fool, the wise too must die!

The Pleasure Is Mine

Joe Stowell

I refused my heart no pleasure. . . . Everything was
meaningless, a chasing after the wind.

Ecclesiastes 2:10–11

I always look forward to summer. The warm sunshine, baseball, beaches, and barbecues are pleasures that bring joy after a long, cold winter. But pleasure-seeking isn't just seasonal. Don't we all enjoy good food, engaging conversation, and a crackling fire?

The desire for pleasure isn't wrong. God has built us for it. Paul reminds us that God "richly provides us with everything for our enjoyment" (1 Timothy 6:17). Other passages welcome us to the healthy pleasure of food, friends, and the intimacy of a marriage relationship. But thinking that we can find lasting pleasure in people and things is ultimately an empty pursuit.

Ultimate pleasure is not found in the short-lived thrills our world offers, but rather in the long-term joy from a deepening intimacy with our Lord. King Solomon learned this the hard way. "I refused my heart no pleasure," he admitted (Ecclesiastes 2:10). But after his pleasure-seeking spree, he concluded: "Everything was meaningless, a chasing after the wind" (v. 11). It's no wonder he warned, "Whoever loves pleasure will become poor" (Proverbs 21:17).

What we are really looking for is satisfied only in a fulfilling and growing relationship with Jesus. Pursue Him and taste His delights!

> What pursuit or gift are you particularly grateful for right now? Take time to thank God for it, listening for how God responds to your words.

A Time for Tearing Down

Warning: it gets worse before it gets better! The first three units of Ecclesiastes—see Structure below—are largely negative.[3] Through his educational method, the Teacher wants to demolish the faulty foundations on which we find meaning and purpose apart from God. Only then can he instruct us on how to build our lives on the bedrock of God's ways and wisdom (12:13), which he explores in the book's second half, particularly in the book's last three chapters.[4]

Finally, while reading Ecclesiastes, expect to be disoriented. The book isn't linear! Instead, you are invited on a journey with Solomon: experiencing his larger-than-life pursuits, failures, and contradictions with him—allowing you to come face-to-face with your own questions. Through the discord, you'll feel the ache of human existence: how indescribable beauty is interspliced with suffering, moments of clarity with confusion, and glimpses of joy with uncertainty.

Ecclesiastes: Structure

While confusing (or seemingly nonexistent) to us as Western readers, the structure of Ecclesiastes would have made more sense to its original Hebrew audience. According to Old Testament scholar David Dorsey, Ecclesiastes likely has a *chiastic structure*, a plotline common in Hebrew literature. In contrast with Western literature—where the turning point of a story is at a book's end—the turning point of a chiastic plotline is at a book's center. For example, in Ecclesiastes, the book's parts are symmetrically clustered around the book's middle part, which reveals the big idea of Ecclesiastes—to "fear God" (5:7).

The Book of Ecclesiastes: Outline[5]

Introduction (author mentioned in third person)—1:1

  A Brevity and insignificance of life (poem)—1:2–11

    B Wisdom's failure to discover life's meaning (autobiographical)—1:12–2:26

      C Poem about time—3:1–15

        D Center: Fear God!—3:16–6:12

      C′ Poem about time revisited—7:1–14

    B′ Wisdom's failure revisited (autobiographical)—7:15–10:19

  A′ Life's brevity revisited (poem and practical advice)—10:20–12:8

Conclusion: Fear God! (author mentioned in third person)—12:9–14

Day 5

Ecclesiastes 2:17–26

¹⁷ *So I hated life, because the work that is done under the sun was grievous to me. All of it is meaningless, a chasing after the wind.* ¹⁸ *I hated all the things I had toiled for under the sun, because I must leave them to the one who comes after me.* ¹⁹ *And who knows whether that person will be wise or foolish? Yet they will have control over all the fruit of my toil into which I have poured my effort and skill under the sun. This too is meaningless.* ²⁰ *So my heart began to despair over all my toilsome labor under the sun.* ²¹ *For a person may labor with wisdom, knowledge and skill, and then they must leave all they own to another who has not toiled for it. This too is meaningless and a great misfortune.* ²² *What do people get for all the toil and anxious striving with which they labor under the sun?* ²³ *All their days their work is grief and pain; even at night their minds do not rest. This too is meaningless.*

²⁴ *A person can do nothing better than to eat and drink and find satisfaction in their own toil. This too, I see, is from the hand of God,* ²⁵ *for without him, who can eat or find enjoyment?* ²⁶ *To the person who pleases him, God gives wisdom, knowledge and happiness, but to the sinner he gives the task of gathering and storing up wealth to hand it over to the one who pleases God. This too is meaningless, a chasing after the wind.*

The Reason to Rest

Kirsten Holmberg

What do people get for all the toil and anxious
striving with which they labor under the sun?

Ecclesiastes 2:22

I f you want to live longer, take a vacation! Forty years after a
study of middle-aged, male executives who each had a risk
of heart disease, researchers in Helsinki, Finland, followed
up with their study participants. The scientists discovered something they hadn't been looking for in their original findings: the
death rate was lower among those who had taken time off for
vacations.

Work is a necessary part of life—a part God appointed to us
even before our relationship with Him was fractured in Genesis 3.
The author of Ecclesiastes wrote of the seeming meaninglessness
of work—recognizing its "anxious striving" and "grief and pain"
(Ecclesiastes 2:22–23). Even when people are not actively working, he says their "minds do not rest" because they're thinking
about what still needs to be done (v. 23).

We too might at times feel like we're "chasing after the wind"
(v. 17) and grow frustrated by our inability to "finish" our work.
But when we remember that God is part of our labor—our purpose—we can both work hard and take time to rest. We can trust
Him to be our Provider, for He's the giver of all things. Solomon
acknowledges that "without him, who can eat or find enjoyment?" (v. 25). Perhaps by reminding ourselves of that truth, we
can work diligently for Him (Colossians 3:23) and also allow
ourselves times of rest.

How can you invite God into your labors?
How might you allow Him to be
your satisfaction even when your work
isn't "finished"?

Dead Ends

Ecclesiastes is the Teacher's quest to discover meaning and purpose apart from God. Like a skilled investigator, the Teacher painstakingly pursues leads for life's meaning. In Ecclesiastes 1:12–2:26, he personally recounts his relentless exploration of seven pathways to significance, ultimately exposing each as a dead end.[6]

1. The pursuit of the philosopher (1:12–15)
2. The pursuit of wisdom (1:16–18)
3. The pursuit of pleasure (2:1–2)
4. The pursuit of escapism (2:3)
5. The pursuit of success (2:4–11)
6. The pursuit of common-sense living (2:12–16)
7. The pursuit of leaving a legacy (2:17–23)

Through his compelling narrative, the Teacher calls us to let go of the futile attempt to find ultimate meaning "under the sun" and, instead, to live humbly before God—enjoying His good gifts (2:24–26)!

Day 6

Ecclesiastes 3:1–8

¹ *There is a time for everything,*
   and a season for every activity under the heavens:

² *a time to be born and a time to die,*
a time to plant and a time to uproot,
³ *a time to kill and a time to heal,*
a time to tear down and a time to build,
⁴ *a time to weep and a time to laugh,*
a time to mourn and a time to dance,
⁵ *a time to scatter stones and a time to gather them,*
a time to embrace and a time to refrain from embracing,
⁶ *a time to search and a time to give up,*
a time to keep and a time to throw away,
⁷ *a time to tear and a time to mend,*
a time to be silent and a time to speak,
⁸ *a time to love and a time to hate,*
a time for war and a time for peace.

A Season for Everything

Poh Fang Chia

There is a time for everything, and a season for every
activity under the heavens.

Ecclesiastes 3:1

If you're like me, you've struggled with having to say no to taking on a
new responsibility—especially if it's for a good cause and directly related
to helping others. We may have sound reasons for carefully selecting our
priorities. Yet sometimes, by not agreeing to do more, we may feel guilty or
we may think that somehow we have failed in our walk of faith.

But according to Ecclesiastes 3:1–8, wisdom recognizes that everything
in life has its own season—in human activities as in the realm of nature.
"There is a time for everything, and a season for every activity under the
heavens" (3:1).

Perhaps you are getting married or becoming a parent for the first time.
Maybe you are leaving school and entering the workforce, or moving from
full-time work to retirement. As we move from season to season, our priorities change. We may need to put aside what we did in the past and funnel
our energy into something else.

When life brings changes in our circumstances and obligations, we must
responsibly and wisely discern what kind of commitments we should make,
seeking in whatever we do to "do it all for the glory of God" (1 Corinthians
10:31). Proverbs 3:6 promises that as we acknowledge Him in all our ways,
He will guide us in the way we should go.

> What decisions are you navigating
> in this season? As you pray, invite God
> into your decision-making process.

About: Poem

Today's passage is well-known, especially considering its popular song adaptation: "Turn! Turn! Turn!" first recorded in 1959. Ecclesiastes 3:1 indicates that what follows is a comprehensive picture of life: "There is a time for everything, and a season for every activity." Edward Curtis, in his commentary on Ecclesiastes, notes that the author uses a *merism*, where two opposites (such as weeping and laughing) "imply all the activities that lie between the two poles."[7] Here we also see two pairs of seven. Because seven can be a symbol of completion, the fourteen pairs suggest the poem encompasses the full scope of life events.

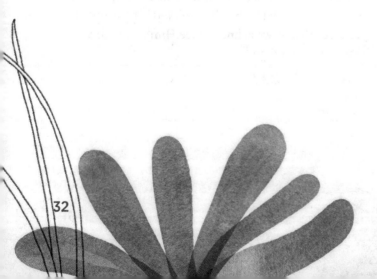

Prayer

My great Father, my heart longs for seasons of blessing,
For those times to birth and plant and heal and build.

I long for the days of laughter, dancing, embracing, and mending.

And yet, in the seasons of death and weeping and searching
and silence,
I too often forget that You are here.

Forgive me for wanting what You have not given.
Teach me thankfulness for what You have.

Instruct my heart to love You and tell of Your love,
No matter the season.

Amen and amen.

Day 7

Ecclesiastes 3:9–11

⁹ What do workers gain from their toil? ¹⁰ I have seen the burden God has laid on the human race. ¹¹ He has made everything beautiful in its time. He has also set eternity in the human heart; yet no one can fathom what God has done from beginning to end.

Enjoying Beauty

Patricia Raybon

He has made everything beautiful in its time.

Ecclesiastes 3:11

The painting caught my eye like a beacon. Displayed along a long hallway in a big city hospital, its deep pastel hues and Navajo Native American figures were so arresting I stopped to marvel and stare. "Look at that," I said to my husband, Dan.

He was walking ahead but I hesitated, bypassing other paintings on the wall to gaze only at that one. "Beautiful," I whispered.

Many things in life are beautiful indeed. Master paintings. Scenic vistas. Inspired crafts. But so is a child's smile. A friend's hello. A robin's blue egg. A seashell's strong ridges. To relieve the burdens life can bring, "[God] has made everything beautiful in its time" (Ecclesiastes 3:11). In such beauty, Bible scholars explain, we get a glimpse of the perfection of God's creation—including the glory of His perfect rule to come.

We can only imagine such perfection, so God grants us a foretaste through life's beauty. In this way, God "has also set eternity in the human heart" (v. 11). Some days life looks drab and futile. But God mercifully provides moments of beauty to ponder.

The artist of the painting I admired, Gerard Curtis Delano, understood that. "God [gave] me a talent to create beauty," he once said, "and this is what He wanted me to do."

Seeing such beauty, how can we respond? We can thank God for eternity to come while pausing to enjoy the glory we already see.

Searching for a Larger Purpose

Essential to the elegance of Ecclesiastes is the author's use of poetic devices, including repetition. This sets a mood of relentless, mundane monotony. Life drags on and on, to no real purpose. Happily, Solomon finds beauty, too, as we see in the eloquent parallelism of 3:1–8 about life's seasons.

Just as quickly, however, this beauty encounters a stark question, one that echoes 1:3: "What do workers gain from their toil?" (3:9). And then—with simple imagery Solomon turns on the light. God has "set eternity in the human heart" (3:11). He recognizes that we can never fully comprehend this life and what God is doing, yet the fact that we are aware of something larger than ourselves gives us hope. We're compelled to continue our search for that larger purpose—our journey toward the Light of the world.

> What beauty in the world causes you to respond with awe? How does beauty reflect God?

word study

Eternity

[ˈolam] (v. 11)

The Hebrew word ˈolam (eternity) refers to the far distant future or past, which is beyond our experience or understanding. When we glimpse beauty in nature, in relationships, in laughter—and long for more—we're experiencing the truth of Ecclesiastes 3:11: "[God] has made everything beautiful in its time. He has also set eternity in the human heart." In the beginning, God made a perfect, timeless world; but with sin, creation was subjected to a "bondage to decay" (Romans 8:21). Paul wrote that we, with all creation, "groan inwardly" for eternity, for the new creation when all is restored and we're forever in God's presence (vv. 22–23).

Day 8

Ecclesiastes 3:12–15

¹² *I know that there is nothing better for people than to be happy and to do good while they live.* ¹³ *That each of them may eat and drink, and find satisfaction in all their toil—this is the gift of God.* ¹⁴ *I know that everything God does will endure forever; nothing can be added to it and nothing taken from it. God does it so that people will fear him.*

¹⁵ *Whatever is has already been,*
and what will be has been before;
and God will call the past to account.

What's the Occasion?

Tim Gustafson

Everything God does will endure forever.
Ecclesiastes 3:14

Four-year-old Asher's gleeful face peeked out from beneath his favorite hooded sweatshirt—his alligator-head sweatshirt, complete with plush jaws that seemed to swallow his head! His mom's heart sank. She wanted the family to make a good impression as they visited a family they hadn't seen in a long time.

"Oh, Hon," she said, "that may not be appropriate for the occasion."

"Of course it is!" Asher protested brightly.

"Hmm, and what occasion might that be?" she asked.

Asher replied, "You know. Life!" He got to wear the shirt.

That joyful boy already grasps the truth of Ecclesiastes 3:12: "There is nothing better for people than to be happy and to do good while they live." Ecclesiastes can seem depressing and is often misunderstood because it's written from a human perspective, not God's. King Solomon asked, "What do workers gain from their toil?" (v. 9). Yet throughout the book we catch glimpses of hope. Solomon also wrote: "That each of [us] may eat and drink, and find satisfaction in all [our] toil—this is the gift of God" (v. 13).

We serve a God who gives us good things to enjoy. Everything He does "will endure forever" (v. 14). As we acknowledge Him and follow His loving commands, He infuses our lives with purpose, meaning, and joy.

Theme: Enjoying God's Gifts

A big theme of Ecclesiastes is that even without understanding all the *whys*, we can still enjoy God's good gifts. Here the Teacher implores us to do just that (3:12). He calls us to seize the day (*carpe diem*). In 2:24 he notes there is nothing better than to "eat and drink and find satisfaction in [our] own toil." That theme is echoed in 3:22; 5:18; 8:15; 9:7–9; and 11:8–9. In 7:14 he says, "When times are good, be happy."

If Ecclesiastes were a song, such *carpe diem* sections would provide the joyful countermelody to the main chorus of Ecclesiastes, that *everything is meaningless.* They demonstrate the Teacher's belief in God and his perspective that joy (3:12), love (9:9), work (5:18–19), and feasting are good gifts from our Creator (3:13).

> What areas of your life are life giving?
> What about those that are discouraging
> or draining? Talk to God about them,
> listening for His encouragement, comfort,
> and guidance.

word study

Toil

['*amal*] (v. 13)

Here we encounter another term drenched in monotony—*toil* (Hebrew '*amal*). The word occurs first in 1:3 and then throughout the book. It conveys the sense of tiresome, difficult labor and exertion. The repetition of '*amal* throughout Ecclesiastes contributes to the tension the writer creates. On the one hand, he finds everything meaningless. Yet, because God has put eternity in our hearts, we persist in our search for meaning and purpose, and here the Teacher states that purpose: "God does it so that people will fear him" (3:14). This fear is one of reverential respect. It is also a fear that urges us to find life's true meaning. The book of Ecclesiastes will end with a focus on this very theme: "Fear God and keep his commandments" (12:13).

Day 9

Ecclesiastes 3:16–22

¹⁶ *And I saw something else under the sun:*

> *In the place of judgment—wickedness was there,*
> > *in the place of justice—wickedness was there.*

¹⁷ *I said to myself,*

> *"God will bring into judgment*
> > *both the righteous and the wicked,*
> *for there will be a time for every activity,*
> > *a time to judge every deed."*

¹⁸ *I also said to myself, "As for humans, God tests them so that they may see that they are like the animals.* ¹⁹ *Surely the fate of human beings is like that of the animals; the same fate awaits them both: As one dies, so dies the other. All have the same breath; humans have no advantage over animals. Everything is meaningless.* ²⁰ *All go to the same place; all come from dust, and to dust all return.* ²¹ *Who knows if the human spirit rises upward and if the spirit of the animal goes down into the earth?"*

²² *So I saw that there is nothing better for a person than to enjoy their work, because that is their lot. For who can bring them to see what will happen after them?*

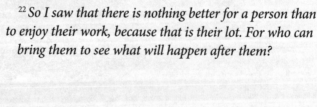

Until God Judges

Patricia Raybon

There will be a time . . . to judge every deed.
Ecclesiastes 3:17

For eight years, Morris Kaberia languished in a Kenyan prison. A former police officer, he was accused of stealing a cell phone and credit card—a bogus charge for not paying a supervisor's bribe, he insisted. Then came his sentence. Death by hanging. "I just saw black. Darkness everywhere," he said.

He found light again, however, in an unusual nonprofit program—Justice Defenders—started by a young London lawyer to help prisoners become lawyers and paralegals themselves. Then they can combat injustice from within justice systems. Acquitted after appealing his own case, Kaberia went right back to prison to help others, working full-time for the program that helped him gain a law degree while behind bars.

As Solomon observed, even in a place of justice, "wickedness was there" (Ecclesiastes 3:16). "Under the sun there is evil in the courtroom. Yes, even the courts of law are corrupt!" (v. 16 NLT). Seeing this contradiction, Solomon asked how God's perfect plan for humankind can flourish when so much injustice exists, even in places intended for justice—our court systems.

Indeed, millions of prisoners worldwide have been denied fair trials, and many fight this injustice. But God, in the fullness of His time, "will bring into judgment both the righteous and the wicked, for there will be a time for every activity, a time to judge every deed" (v. 17). May we be assured in the meantime that God, the Final Judge, will right every wrong for good.

Where have you witnessed injustice?

Reality: Injustice

A conundrum confronts the Teacher in his quest for meaning: why is there injustice? "In the place of judgment—wickedness was there" (3:16). He sees a similar fate awaiting humanity and the animals. Ultimately, we all go to the grave (v. 19). Such raw honesty in the pages of the Bible gives us permission to express our anguish over the injustice and meaningless suffering we see in this world.

Yet the Teacher also saw how "God will bring into judgment both the righteous and the wicked" (v. 17)—a conviction that prevents him from slipping into total despondency.

To what injustice are you feeling led to respond? Ask God about the timing.

word study

Justice

[*mishpat*] (vv. 16, 17)

The Hebrew word *mishpat*—justice—is a central scriptural theme. Human beings were meant to treat others fairly as those made in God's image. Too often, however, power imbalances give some unequal benefits like wealth while leaving others vulnerable to mistreatment. In this context, *mishpat* in Scripture is often focused on restoring fairness and equity when it has been violated. God's people, followers of a just God (Deuteronomy 10:18) are called to devote themselves to "seek justice" and "defend the oppressed" (Isaiah 1:17).

The Teacher in Ecclesiastes was tormented by how widespread injustice was. The corrupt and greedy held the power to cruelly exploit the vulnerable (4:1; 5:8–10). And the law court, the very places meant to restore *mishpat*, was doing the opposite (3:16; 5:8). While the Teacher found some comfort in God's judgment (3:17), he struggled with the reality of death prior to *mishpat*'s restoration (v. 19).

Day 10

Ecclesiastes 4:1–8

¹ *Again I looked and saw all the oppression that was taking place under the sun:*

> *I saw the tears of the oppressed—*
> > *and they have no comforter;*
> *power was on the side of their oppressors—*
> > *and they have no comforter.*
> ² *And I declared that the dead,*
> > *who had already died,*
> *are happier than the living,*
> > *who are still alive.*
> ³ *But better than both*
> > *is the one who has never been born,*
> *who has not seen the evil*
> > *that is done under the sun.*

⁴ *And I saw that all toil and all achievement spring from one person's envy of another. This too is meaningless, a chasing after the wind.*

⁵ *Fools fold their hands*
   and ruin themselves.
⁶ *Better one handful with tranquillity*
   than two handfuls with toil
   and chasing after the wind.

⁷ *Again I saw something meaningless under the sun:*

⁸ *There was a man all alone;*
   he had neither son nor brother.
There was no end to his toil,
   yet his eyes were not content with his wealth.
"For whom am I toiling," he asked,
   "and why am I depriving myself of enjoyment?"
This too is meaningless—
   a miserable business!

Always Enough

Xochitl Dixon

There was a man all alone. . . . There was no end to his toil, yet his eyes were not content with his wealth. . . . This too is meaningless.

Ecclesiastes 4:8

After another late night in the office, Angelique crawled into her king-size bed and picked up her cell phone. No messages. No missed calls. Did she expect anything different? Over the years, she'd scrapped too many weekend plans and botched too many relationships as she worked harder for her *next* promotion. Placing her phone on top of her dusty Bible, she turned off the light, pulled the duvet under her chin, and prepared to spend another birthday alone in her quiet dream house. She wept into her satin pillowcase. Was meeting her #lifegoals worth the sacrifices she'd made? Would she ever have enough? Would she ever feel like she was enough?

The futile search for significance and satisfaction through work, status, and accomplishments has consumed humankind for centuries, often at the expense of our relationships with God and others. The writer of Ecclesiastes affirmed the pointlessness of "all toil and all achievement" that "spring from one person's envy of another" (Ecclesiastes 4:4).

Living in a success-obsessed culture breeds comparison and competition, which lead to seeking approval and self-worth through prestige. However, the Bible says that "one handful with tranquility"—peace through contentment—is better than having more only to keep needing more (v. 6). Without relationships, all the riches and glory in the world would never be enough (v. 8). As God secures our significance and satisfaction in the surety of His love, He promises that He is always enough.

When have you struggled with not having or not being enough?

How has God's love for you changed the way you determine the value of yourself and others?

word study

Chasing after the Wind

[*re'ut ruah; ra'yon ruah*] (v. 17)

The phrase "chasing after the wind," which is found only in Ecclesiastes, appears nine times (1:14, 17; 2:11, 17, 26; 4:4, 6, 16; 6:9). To chase after the wind is a pointless, futile activity (in most references of the phrase, it's paired with *hebel*—translated "meaningless"). No matter how hard we try, we can never catch the wind. The Teacher begins the book with the theme: "I have seen all the things that are done under the sun; all of them are meaningless, a chasing after the wind" (1:14). In our passage, he applies the phrase to ambition (4:4). It's disheartening for him to realize our desire to succeed often springs from the envy of others' achievements.

Prayer

My dear Father, teach me to want what You want.
I see what others have,
I hear what others achieve,
I know what others do,
And my heart grows heavy with the strangling lies that envy tells.

Teach me to want what You want.
To rejoice with those who rejoice, even though I feel the
sting of suffering.
To weep with those who weep, even though I know the
sweetness of satisfaction.

Make me a balm to others, so they may know Your love.
And the love of Your Son.
And the hope of Your Spirit.

Amen.

Day 11

Ecclesiastes 4:9–16

⁹ Two are better than one,
  because they have a good return for their labor:
¹⁰ If either of them falls down,
  one can help the other up.
But pity anyone who falls
  and has no one to help them up.
¹¹ Also, if two lie down together, they will keep warm.
  But how can one keep warm alone?
¹² Though one may be overpowered,
  two can defend themselves.
A cord of three strands is not quickly broken.

¹³ Better a poor but wise youth than an old but foolish king who no longer knows how to heed a warning. ¹⁴ The youth may have come from prison to the kingship, or he may have been born in poverty within his kingdom. ¹⁵ I saw that all who lived and walked under the sun followed the youth, the king's successor. ¹⁶ There was no end to all the people who were before them. But those who came later were not pleased with the successor. This too is meaningless, a chasing after the wind.

The Saddest Goose

Adam R. Holz

Though one may be overpowered, two can defend themselves. A cord of three strands is not quickly broken.

Ecclesiastes 4:12

Why is there a football in the parking lot? I wondered. But as I got closer, I realized the greyish lump wasn't a football: it was a *goose*—the saddest Canada goose I'd ever seen.

Geese often congregate on the lawn near my workplace in the spring and fall. But today there was only one, its neck arced back and its head tucked beneath a wing. Where are your buddies? I thought. Poor thing was all alone. It looked so lonely, I wanted to give it a hug. (Note: don't try this.)

I've rarely seen a goose completely alone like my lonesome feathered friend. Geese are notably communal, flying in a V formation to deflect the wind. They're made to be together.

As human beings, we were created for community too (see Genesis 2:18). And in Ecclesiastes 4:10, Solomon describes how vulnerable we are when we're alone: "Pity anyone who falls and has no one to help them up." There's strength in numbers, he added, for "though one may be overpowered, two can defend themselves. A cord of three strands is not quickly broken" (v. 12).

This is just as true for us spiritually as it is physically. God never intended for us to "fly" alone, vulnerably isolated. We need relationships with each other for encouragement, refreshment, and growth (see also 1 Corinthians 12:21). Together, we can stand firm when life's head winds gust our way. Together.

> What kinds of circumstances tempt you to go it alone?

> What would healthy community look like to you?

Relationships

Ecclesiastes 4:8–12 stresses the importance of relationships. We weren't meant to be alone, and that's why, at the beginning, God created Eve and Adam for each other (Genesis 1:27; 2:20–23). Two or more in right relationship to each other work better together than one of us on our own, according to the author. For example, on our own, we may wonder, why work hard when we have no one to work for (Ecclesiastes 4:8). When two of us work together, the workload is lightened, and someone is there if we are injured or need help (vv. 9–10, 12). Another person offers companionship and warmth (v. 11). As the author wrote so eloquently, "A cord of three strands is not quickly broken" (v. 12).

The apostle Paul defines what a right relationship should be: union with Christ first and foremost, like-mindedness, and treating each other with love, humbly valuing others above self (Philippians 2:1–4).

Prayer

Thank You, Father, for Your kindness to me,
That though sometimes I feel the sting of isolation,
You have not left me alone.

Teach me to love the people around me,
To carry their burdens,
To bear their pain,
To touch their sadness,
So that the hope of Your presence is present in their lives.

May I be the second that betters their one.
As Your Son and Your Spirit have enlivened me,
Teach me to enliven others.

For Your name alone,
Amen.

Day 12

Ecclesiastes 5:1–7

[1] *Guard your steps when you go to the house of God. Go near to listen rather than to offer the sacrifice of fools, who do not know that they do wrong.*

> [2] *Do not be quick with your mouth,*
>   *do not be hasty in your heart*
>   *to utter anything before God.*
> *God is in heaven*
>   *and you are on earth,*
>   *so let your words be few.*
> [3] *A dream comes when there are many cares,*
>   *and many words mark the speech of a fool.*

[4] *When you make a vow to God, do not delay to fulfill it. He has no pleasure in fools; fulfill your vow.* [5] *It is better not to make a vow than to make one and not fulfill it.* [6] *Do not let your mouth lead you into sin. And do not protest to the temple messenger, "My vow was a mistake." Why should God be angry at what you say and destroy the work of your hands?* [7] *Much dreaming and many words are meaningless. Therefore fear God.*

The Last Word

Amy Boucher Pye

*Do not be quick with your mouth, do not
be hasty in your heart.*
Ecclesiastes 5:2

One day during a university philosophy class, a student made some inflammatory remarks about the professor's views. To the surprise of the other students, the teacher thanked him and moved on to another comment. When he was asked later why he didn't respond to the student, he said, "I'm practicing the discipline of not having to have the last word."

This teacher loved and honored God, and he wanted to embody a humble spirit as he reflected this love. His words remind me of another Teacher—this one from long ago, who wrote the book of Ecclesiastes. Although not addressing how to handle an angry person, he said that when we approach the Lord, we should guard our steps and "go near to listen" rather than being quick with our mouths and hasty in our hearts. By doing so we acknowledge that God is the Lord and we are those whom He has created (Ecclesiastes 5:1–2).

How do you approach God? If you sense that your attitude could use some adjustment, why not spend some time considering the majesty and greatness of the Lord? When we ponder His unending wisdom, power, and presence, we can feel awed by His overflowing love for us. With this posture of humility, we too need not have the last word.

> Recall a time in which you were in awe of God's majesty, beauty, or kindness. Meditate on that experience of God's character and attributes.

Worshiping God

In the midst of so much cynical thinking, the Teacher surprises us with wise counsel in this text. Put simply, his counsel would seem to be "know your place." When we come before the living God, it is easy to forget that He is the Lord of the universe and does not exist to respond to our foolishness or whims. Hence, the challenge to "guard your steps" as you approach the place of worship is an important reminder of the greatness of the God we serve (5:1). He is well able to meet our needs, but he is also well worthy of our love, trust, and worship.

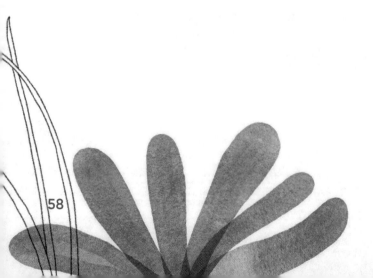

word study

Fear

[*yirah*] (v. 7)

Most of Ecclesiastes narrates Solomon's spectacular failure to find meaning apart from God. In his unsuccessful quest, Solomon showcases the need for us to abandon our search to find lasting significance in the here and now. Instead, we're called to surrender to the mystery of God's ways—that is, to *fear God*. To *fear God* (in Hebrew, *fear* is *yirah*) means to wholeheartedly reverence and obediently trust in our Creator.

Proverbs calls the fear of the Lord "the beginning of wisdom" (9:10), and Ecclesiastes affirms this message by placing the advice to *fear God* at prominent positions in this Wisdom book, such as here at the book's center (5:7) and at the conclusion (12:13). In the author's parting wisdom (12:13), the exhortation to *fear God* invites us to humbly entrust ourselves to the one who sees the "big picture," even if we can't.

Day 13

Ecclesiastes 5:8–12

[8] *If you see the poor oppressed in a district, and justice and rights denied, do not be surprised at such things; for one official is eyed by a higher one, and over them both are others higher still.* [9] *The increase from the land is taken by all; the king himself profits from the fields.*

[10] *Whoever loves money never has enough;*
whoever loves wealth is never satisfied with their income.
This too is meaningless.

[11] *As goods increase,*
so do those who consume them.
And what benefit are they to the owners
except to feast their eyes on them?

[12] *The sleep of a laborer is sweet,*
whether they eat little or much,
but as for the rich, their abundance
permits them no sleep.

You Can't Take It with You

Tim Gustafson

The sleep of a laborer is sweet, whether they
eat little or much, but as for the rich, their abundance
permits them no sleep.

Ecclesiastes 5:12

As the jet accelerated down the runway, its cargo shifted rearward, causing the plane's nose to rise. In an awful instant, the aircraft left the ground—too soon. Barely aloft, the plane tipped back on its tail, tilted sharply right, and pitched earthward. Everyone on board the Tupolev Tu-104 was killed—including sixteen admirals and generals departing a leadership conference.

The official investigation reports only that the plane had been loaded unevenly, but it appears the cargo well exceeded the jetliner's limits. Much of it was luxury items purchased by those high-ranking officers, who had demanded the goods be loaded and threatened the crew when they protested.

Greed isn't a characteristic of only the powerful. It's an inherent trait in all of us, and Solomon knew it. He noted, "Whoever loves money never has enough; whoever loves wealth is never satisfied with their income" (Ecclesiastes 5:10). We will never attain fulfillment through material wealth. The secret to a satisfied life instead lies in contentment. "The sleep of a laborer is sweet," the Teacher observed, "whether they eat little or much, but as for the rich, their abundance permits them no sleep" (v. 12).

We can't pull rank on the laws of physics; neither can we find satisfaction in the things we accumulate. The writer of Hebrews sums it up for us: "Keep your lives free from the love of money and be content with what you have" (13:5).

> In what ways do you pursue happiness
> or fulfillment? According to today's
> reading, what might you need to change?

Wealth in Ecclesiastes

The author of Ecclesiastes warns against the love of money. People who love money are never satisfied with what they have (5:10). It can be a compulsion that leads to an unquenchable desire and striving for more, including hoarding and depriving others (vv. 11–14). The apostle Paul agrees: "The love of money is a root of all kinds of evil" (1 Timothy 6:10). Moreover, for all our labor, we can lose everything we've worked for with one misfortune; and we can't take it with us when we die (Ecclesiastes 5:15–16; 1 Timothy 6:7). Yet, the Teacher concludes, "wealth and possessions, and the ability to enjoy them" are a gift from God (Ecclesiastes 5:19). If we're blessed monetarily, it's a gift meant to be enjoyed and shared with others. No matter how little or much we have, "Godliness with contentment is great gain" (1 Timothy 6:6).

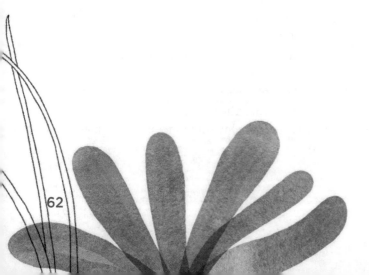

Prayer

Great Father, whose ear holds the cry of the infant,
Whose hands hold the volume of the sea,
Whose eyes hold every thread of time,
I thank You.

Thank You that You see my needs, hold my life, and
hear my requests.

Teach my heart to be content with what You have given me.
Teach my hands to use Your gifts for others.
And teach my soul to trust when there doesn't seem to be enough.

May the world thus know the God who sees, holds,
and hears all people.

May that be enough for me today.
Amen.

Day 14

Ecclesiastes 5:13–17

¹³ *I have seen a grievous evil under the sun:*

> *wealth hoarded to the harm of its owners,*
> ¹⁴ *or wealth lost through some misfortune,*
> *so that when they have children*
> *there is nothing left for them to inherit.*
> ¹⁵ *Everyone comes naked from their mother's womb,*
> *and as everyone comes, so they depart.*
> *They take nothing from their toil*
> *that they can carry in their hands.*

¹⁶ *This too is a grievous evil:*

> *As everyone comes, so they depart,*
> *and what do they gain,*
> *since they toil for the wind?*
> ¹⁷ *All their days they eat in darkness,*
> *with great frustration, affliction and anger.*

Stockpiling or Storing?

Jennifer Benson Schuldt

As everyone comes, so they depart.
Ecclesiastes 5:16

Rugs, lamps, a washer and dryer, even the food in the cupboards—everything was for sale! My husband and I stopped at an estate sale one day and wandered through the house, overwhelmed by the volume of belongings. Dish sets littered the dining room table. Christmas decorations filled the front hallway. Tools, toy cars, board games, and vintage dolls crowded the garage. When we left, I wondered if the home-owners were moving, if they desperately needed money, or if they had passed away.

This reminded me of these words from Ecclesiastes: "As every-one comes, so they depart" (5:16). We're born empty-handed and we leave the world the same way. The stuff we buy, orga-nize, and store is ours only for a while—and it's all in a state of decay. Moths munch through our clothes; even gold and silver may not hold their value (James 5:2–3). Sometimes "wealth [is] lost through some misfortune" (Ecclesiastes 5:14), and our kids don't get to enjoy our possessions after we're gone.

Stockpiling possessions in the here and now is foolish, because we can't take anything with us when we die. What's important is a proper attitude toward what we have and how we use what God has given. That way we'll be storing up our treasure where it belongs—in heaven.

> Jesus said to "store up for yourselves treasures in heaven" (Matthew 6:19-20). What does that look like in your own life?

Futility of Wealth

The Teacher continues his theme of wealth's inadequacy and the futility of "toil" (5:15). What good is it to save money? We can lose everything and have nothing to leave to our children. We hear an echo from another Wisdom book in the Bible. Job, after losing all he had, said, "Naked I came from my mother's womb, and naked I will depart" (Job 1:21; compare Ecclesiastes 5:15). The Teacher asserts that we "toil for the wind" (5:16). But Jesus advised, "Do not store up for yourselves treasures on earth. . . . Store up for yourselves treasures in heaven" (Matthew 6:19–20).

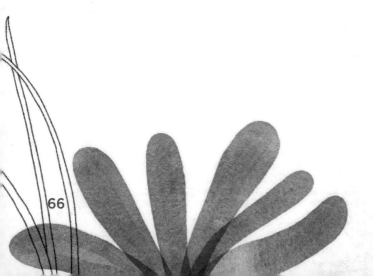

Prayer

I cannot change the world, but You can change me, dear Father.

I fear too often that I will not have enough,
Enough food,
Enough time,
Enough money,
So I race to collect more.

Work in my heart and my mind, and teach me to trust,
To trust that You will provide what I need,
That You can satisfy my heart,
That You will fill my life with hope.

Change me, Father, so that I can give rather than gather,
And be a blessing to those who are in need.

Amen.

Day 15

Ecclesiastes 5:18–20

[18] *This is what I have observed to be good: that it is appropriate for a person to eat, to drink and to find satisfaction in their toilsome labor under the sun during the few days of life God has given them—for this is their lot.* [19] *Moreover, when God gives someone wealth and possessions, and the ability to enjoy them, to accept their lot and be happy in their toil—this is a gift of God.* [20] *They seldom reflect on the days of their life, because God keeps them occupied with gladness of heart.*

Follow His Lead

Karen Pimpo

This is what I have observed to be good: that it is appropriate for a person to eat, to drink and to find satisfaction in their toilsome labor under the sun during the few days of life God has given them—for this is their lot.

Ecclesiastes 5:18

One of my favorite childhood novels was about a wild horse and a little girl. The untamed mare would buck and kick at anyone who got too close. Its frustrated owner said that whoever could tame the animal could have it. The girl slowly earned its trust through soft words, tender movements, and treats of apples. She tamed the horse with her gentle affection until it consented to peacefully follow her lead.

Sometimes we act like that wild horse, straining at whatever binds us—hurting ourselves and others in the process. Ecclesiastes encourages us to cease striving and accept our "lot in life," our current limitations and opportunities. When we do, we find peace and satisfaction. Note that this does not give us license to maintain the status quo or to ignore what we sense is God's invitation to try something new—there's still work to do! But our Master is gentle, and His burden is light (Matthew 11:29–30).

To find joy in daily living is a gift from God (Ecclesiastes 5:19). Even the routine things of life like eating, drinking, and working are blessings when we decide to find satisfaction in them (v. 18). Embracing our current season helps us avoid anxiety about the past or future. Those who accept their situation "seldom reflect on the days of their life, because God keeps them occupied with gladness of heart" (v. 20). We can faithfully walk ahead as we trust that God is with us.

> In what way have you been straining against your situation in life?

> How can you find joy in spite of your circumstances?

Gifts from God

Solomon wholeheartedly encourages us "to eat, to drink and to find satisfaction [in our pursuits]" (5:18). Enjoyment is the theme of the other *carpe diem* (seize the day!) passages throughout the book: 2:24–26; 3:22; 8:15. A defender of joy, the author of Ecclesiastes invites us to freely embrace life's good things. The secret to the freedom of enjoyment? Not deriving ultimate meaning, satisfaction, or purpose from our pursuits but viewing them as "gift[s]" from God (5:19). When we *fear God* (12:13), the book's conclusion, our pursuits are rightly prioritized (11:9). Derek Kidner writes, "*Fear God* is a call that puts us in our place, and all other fears, hopes, and admiration in their place."[8]

So, take risks! Celebrate joyfully, and often. And make space in your life for awe.

Authorship

Ecclesiastes is the autobiography and reflections of "the Teacher, son of David" (1:1). Christian and Jewish traditions associate him with King Solomon, son of King David. Like the Teacher, Solomon had extraordinary wisdom, incalculable wealth, and outsized pursuits. If Solomon is indeed the Teacher, it's likely that he wrote Ecclesiastes near the end of his life, because he reflects on his regrets and steers readers to entrust themselves to God—something Solomon failed to wholeheartedly do (1 Kings 11:3–4).

Still, many biblical scholars are uncertain about the book's authorship. The Hebrew used reflects a much later period. The Teacher is also introduced in third person (1:1), and this outside source summarizes the book's meaning (7:29; 12:8–14). The book's wisdom, theology, and inspiration are unchanged whoever the narrator.

Day 16

Ecclesiastes 6:1–12

[1] *I have seen another evil under the sun, and it weighs heavily on mankind:* [2] *God gives some people wealth, possessions and honor, so that they lack nothing their hearts desire, but God does not grant them the ability to enjoy them, and strangers enjoy them instead. This is meaningless, a grievous evil.*

[3] *A man may have a hundred children and live many years; yet no matter how long he lives, if he cannot enjoy his prosperity and does not receive proper burial, I say that a stillborn child is better off than he.* [4] *It comes without meaning, it departs in darkness, and in darkness its name is shrouded.* [5] *Though it never saw the sun or knew anything, it has more rest than does that man—* [6] *even if he lives a thousand years twice over but fails to enjoy his prosperity. Do not all go to the same place?*

[7] *Everyone's toil is for their mouth,*
   yet their appetite is never satisfied.
[8] *What advantage have the wise over fools?*
What do the poor gain
   by knowing how to conduct themselves before others?
[9] *Better what the eye sees*
   than the roving of the appetite.
This too is meaningless,
   a chasing after the wind.

[10] *Whatever exists has already been named,*
   and what humanity is has been known;
no one can contend with someone who is stronger.
[11] *The more the words,*
   the less the meaning,
   and how does that profit anyone?

[12] *For who knows what is good for a person in life, during the few and meaningless days they pass through like a shadow? Who can tell them what will happen under the sun after they are gone?*

Who Knows?

Poh Fang Chia

Who knows what is good . . . ?
Ecclesiastes 6:12

According to Chinese legend, when Sai Weng lost one of his prized horses, his neighbor expressed sorrow for his loss. But Sai Weng was unconcerned. He said, "Who knows if it may be a good thing for me?" Surprisingly, the lost horse returned home with another horse. As the neighbor congratulated him, Sai Weng said, "Who knows if it may be a bad thing for me?" As it turned out, his son broke his leg when he rode on the new horse. This seemed like a misfortune, until the army arrived at the village to recruit all able-bodied men to fight in the war. Because of the son's injury, he wasn't recruited, which ultimately may have spared him from death.

This is the story behind the Chinese proverb which teaches that a difficulty can be a blessing in disguise and vice versa. This ancient wisdom has a close parallel in Ecclesiastes 6:12, where the author observes: "Who knows what is good for a person in life?" Indeed, none of us know what the future holds. An adversity might have positive benefits and prosperity might have ill effects.

Each day offers new opportunities, joys, struggles, and suffering. As God's beloved children, we can rest in His sovereignty and trust Him through the good and bad times alike. God has "made the one as well as the other" (7:14). He's with us in all the events in our lives and promises His loving care.

> Can you think of an example where a misfortune turned out to be a blessing?

Emptiness of Life

Here, the Preacher uses shocking language to speak about the emptiness of life—saying a "stillborn child" would be better off than the person who seems successful yet will not be able to enjoy the fruits of their labors. In verse 12, we see his full-blown cynicism as the Preacher refers to a person's days of living as "few and meaningless," their future as bleak and without promise. As Warren Wiersbe wrote, "Wise is the person who takes time to listen to what God has to say. Yes, life may seem to be fleeting and illusive, like a soap bubble ('vain') or a shadow, but 'he who does the will of God abides forever'" (1 John 2:17 NKJV).[9]

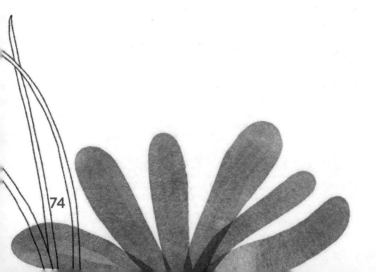

From Self-Reliance to God-Reliance

While in the second half of the book, the Teacher begins offering guidance about how to live well in a flawed, uncertain world, he still tackles some tough topics—some of the most difficult yet! Here, the Teacher uncovers human limitations, exposing the lies we often tell ourselves:[10]

> My life narrative is coherent (you can't ultimately judge what is good or bad; 6:12).
>
> I am in control (randomness and chance will happen to you; 9:11–12; 8:7).
>
> My impact is lasting (you will die; 9:1–10).

By challenging our perceived self-sufficiency, the Teacher helps us arrive at an unflinchingly honest assessment—of ourselves, our limitations, and our vulnerabilities—leading to an awareness of our need for God. Ultimately, Ecclesiastes calls us from self-reliance to God-reliance (12:13).

How can you keep your focus on God in good times as well as in bad times?

Day 17

Ecclesiastes 7:1–6

[1] *A good name is better than fine perfume,*
   and the day of death better than the day of birth.
[2] *It is better to go to a house of mourning*
   than to go to a house of feasting,
for death is the destiny of everyone;
   the living should take this to heart.
[3] *Frustration is better than laughter,*
   because a sad face is good for the heart.
[4] *The heart of the wise is in the house of mourning,*
   but the heart of fools is in the house of pleasure.
[5] *It is better to heed the rebuke of a wise person*
   than to listen to the song of fools.
[6] *Like the crackling of thorns under the pot,*
   so is the laughter of fools.
   This too is meaningless.

Eulogy Virtues

Mike Wittmer

*Death is the destiny of everyone; the living should
take this to heart.*

Ecclesiastes 7:2

My heart is full from attending the funeral of a faithful woman. She wasn't known widely outside her church, neighbors, and friends. But she loved Jesus, her seven children, and her twenty-five grandchildren. She laughed easily, served generously, and could hit a softball a long way.

Ecclesiastes says, "It is better to go to a house of mourning than to go to a house of feasting" (7:2). "The heart of the wise is in the house of mourning" because there we learn what matters most (7:4). *New York Times* columnist David Brooks says there are two kinds of virtues: those that look good on a résumé and those you want said at your funeral. Sometimes these overlap, though often they seem to compete. When in doubt, always choose the eulogy virtues.

The woman in the casket didn't have a résumé, but her children testified that "she rocked Proverbs 31" and its description of a godly woman. She inspired them to love Jesus and care for others. As Paul said, "Follow my example, as I follow the example of Christ" (1 Corinthians 11:1), so they challenged us to imitate their mother's life as she imitated Jesus.

What will be said at your funeral? What do you want said? It's not too late to develop eulogy virtues. Rest in Jesus. His salvation frees us to live for what matters most.

> Are you living out things that will affect your résumé or your eulogy? How would your life change if you lived each day with your eulogy in mind?

Death as Explored in Ecclesiastes

In today's passage, the Teacher discusses a central theme of Ecclesiastes: death (vv. 1–2). According to the Teacher, death is the great leveler. Whether we're good or bad (9:2), wise or reckless (2:12–16), influential or talented (9:11), "death is the destiny of everyone," the Teacher says, and "the living should take this to heart" (7:2). According to the Teacher, death cancels life's meaning: our existence under the sun is absurd largely because death erases us, and everything we've worked so hard to achieve. In a book about human limits, death is the ultimate one.

Knowing this crystalizes the liberating power of Christ's mission: He "destroyed death," freeing us from death's limits (2 Timothy 1:10), enabling all who believe in Him to pass "from death to life" (1 John 3:14).

word study

Good or Better

[*tob*] (vv. 1–14)

In Ecclesiastes 7:1–14, the author presents a series of proverbs or sayings comparing one activity or life experience to another using the word *better* or *good* (Hebrew, *tob*), which occurs eleven times in these verses alone. In the first twelve verses, he explores the question asked earlier: "Who knows what is good for a person . . . ?" (6:12). According to commentator David Dorsey, these verses echo the poem found in 3:1–15 and offer practical guidance in response to such matters as birth and death, feasting and mourning.[11] Despite our limited understanding, the Teacher believes we should seek wiser—or better—ways of living.

Day 18

Ecclesiastes 7:7–12

⁷ *Extortion turns a wise person into a fool,*
and a bribe corrupts the heart.

⁸ *The end of a matter is better than its beginning,*
and patience is better than pride.
⁹ *Do not be quickly provoked in your spirit,*
for anger resides in the lap of fools.

¹⁰ *Do not say, "Why were the old days better than these?"*
For it is not wise to ask such questions.

¹¹ *Wisdom, like an inheritance, is a good thing*
and benefits those who see the sun.
¹² *Wisdom is a shelter*
as money is a shelter,
but the advantage of knowledge is this:
Wisdom preserves those who have it.

The Shelter of Wisdom

Alyson Kieda

Wisdom, like an inheritance, is a good thing and benefits those who see the sun. Wisdom is a shelter as money is a shelter, but the advantage of knowledge is this: Wisdom preserves those who have it.

Ecclesiastes 7:11–12

Shortly after Solomon became king, God came to him in a dream and told him to "ask for whatever" he wanted from Him (1 Kings 3:5). Solomon could have asked for anything, but he wisely responded, "Give your servant a discerning heart to govern your people and to distinguish between right and wrong" (v. 9). His request pleased God, and He blessed him not only with wisdom but also with wealth and honor (vv. 12–13). Solomon understood that "wisdom, like an inheritance, is a good thing" (Ecclesiastes 7:11).

The evidence and news of Solomon's wise decisions quickly spread throughout Israel and beyond. Nowhere could be found his equal. But during his reign, Solomon lost his way. He forgot the source of his wisdom. Unbelievably, he married seven hundred wives. And as he grew older, his many wives led him astray. He foolishly turned away from Israel's God and worshiped their gods. Solomon lost the shelter of wisdom; and after his death, Israel was tragically torn in two (v. 12).

God blesses those who pursue Him—and follow Him wholeheartedly—with wisdom. It's a "good thing" with many "benefits" (v. 11). But when we forget wisdom's source—God—and place anything or anyone above Him, we're no longer wise.

Through a relationship with God and the Spirit's guidance, we gain wisdom (Proverbs 9:10). Let's stay close to the source of wisdom and all that's good.

> In what area of your life do you need God's wisdom and direction? Ask Him, and listen for His response.

On Living Well

Notice that in the second half of the book many of the same themes from the first half crop up—such as wisdom, justice and injustice, and the inclusion of poems. That's because the second half structurally reflects the first half (see Structure, page 25). But unlike the negative treatment of the themes in the first half, the themes in the second are shown in a slightly more positive light.

Take wisdom for example. In the first half, the Teacher laments the failure of wisdom to solve all problems (1:12–16; 2:12–23). But here in 7:11, the Teacher affirms the significance of wisdom: "Wisdom, like an inheritance is a good thing." In the second half, the Teacher still asserts that wisdom can't provide us lasting meaning and purpose, but he tells us it has some inherent value (7:15–22). And he calls us to live with wisdom because it's better than the alternative—being a fool (10:5–19). Increasingly in the second half of Ecclesiastes, the Teacher provides guidance and direction on how to live wisely and abundantly even in an imperfect, broken world.[12]

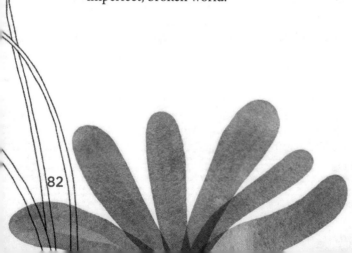

Wisdom Literature in the Bible

Traditionally, the Wisdom Literature of the Old Testament—compilations of wise teachings learned in the crucible of life in a broken world—was listed as Job, Psalms, Proverbs, Song of Songs, and Ecclesiastes. Yet, as we have seen, Ecclesiastes is very different from the other Wisdom books because of its largely cynical and pessimistic worldview. How does it fit? Perhaps as a reminder that God's wisdom is not the only kind of wisdom that can influence our thinking. Read James 3:13–18. There it seems that James codifies what Ecclesiastes exemplifies—that the wisdom that is from above will ever and always be superior to the wisdom of this world and this age.

Seeing the world's wisdom and its outcomes modeled in Ecclesiastes as emptiness and that which has no lasting value should encourage us to embrace God's great wisdom as we live from day to day.

> Identify one way God has guided
> and directed you in the past and thank
> Him for it.

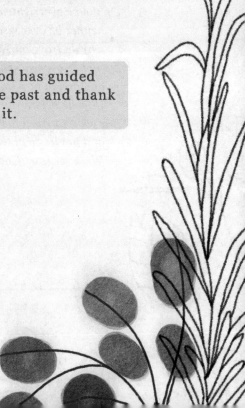

Day 19

Ecclesiastes 7:13–22

¹³ *Consider what God has done:*

Who can straighten
 what he has made crooked?
¹⁴ *When times are good, be happy;*
 but when times are bad, consider this:
God has made the one
 as well as the other.
Therefore, no one can discover
 anything about their future.

¹⁵ *In this meaningless life of mine I have seen both of these:*

the righteous perishing in their righteousness,
 and the wicked living long in their wickedness.
¹⁶ *Do not be overrighteous,*
 neither be overwise—
 why destroy yourself?
¹⁷ *Do not be overwicked,*
 and do not be a fool—
 why die before your time?
¹⁸ *It is good to grasp the one*
 and not let go of the other.
 Whoever fears God will avoid all extremes.

¹⁹ Wisdom makes one wise person more powerful
than ten rulers in a city.

²⁰ Indeed, there is no one on earth who is righteous,
no one who does what is right and never sins.

²¹ Do not pay attention to every word people say,
or you may hear your servant cursing you—
²² for you know in your heart
that many times you yourself have cursed others.

Pour Out Your Heart

Anne Cetas

When times are good, be happy; but when times are bad, consider this: God has made the one as well as the other.

Ecclesiastes 7:14

Life is simply not the same," Beth said after her husband of thirty-two years died. She and Richard had raised two daughters together and enjoyed a loving relationship. She knew she could choose to become bitter toward God about her loss. "Even though I'll never completely understand God's plan, I choose to be 'better' because God is still in control, and He is still good," she says. While still overcome at times by the intensity of her pain and grief, Beth has chosen to remain soft toward God and turn toward Him during those times. A few days before the one-year anniversary of her husband's death, Beth received a beautiful gift of joy from God—another new grandson.

Beth shows us what it looks like to accept the good and bad times in our lives, remembering that both are from God (Ecclesiastes 7:14; see Job 2:10). We like to think that we can control things, but we learn in life that ultimately God is in control. Difficulties give us opportunity to pour out our hearts to Him and learn more of His character and care. We can lean on Scriptures about His strength (Isaiah 12:2), peace (Isaiah 26:3), and compassion (Psalm 116:5) to help us grow in our trust.

Some days look messy as they're mixed with difficulties and joys from God's hand. But those are times to learn to depend on His grace as we struggle deeply and yet rejoice freely—all with Him walking alongside us.

> What might it mean for you to remember that both the good and the bad are from God?

Do Not Be Overrighteous . . .

Ecclesiastes 7:13–14 concludes a collection of proverbs (vv. 1–14) and launches the next section. The Teacher urges us to "consider what God has done" (v. 13) but then returns his gaze to this life only. Again, he declares life meaningless (v. 15). But what does he mean with his warning against being "overrighteous," or "overwise," or "overwicked" (vv. 16–18)? Is a little wickedness acceptable? He may mean that we are to avoid self-righteous hypocrisy. Or perhaps we shouldn't concern ourselves with striving for perfection. The Teacher notes that nobody "does what is right and never sins" (v. 20). Solomon's father David put it more strongly: "The LORD looks down from heaven on all mankind to see if there are any who understand, any who seek God. All have turned away, all have become corrupt; there is no one who does good, not even one" (Psalm 14:2–3).

If you're in a season of trial, express the reality of your pain to God, while clinging to His goodness, compassion, strength, and peace. How does God respond to you?

Prayer

Father in heaven, hear my request this day.

I do not know what I will face in each coming hour.
I expect the good and experience the bad,
Or fear the bad and suspect the good.

And yet, never do they surprise You.

Hold me by the hand when I walk through the hard times.
The pain is often too much for me,
And so I need Your comfort.

Lift my head and hands when I walk into blessing.
The joy is often hard for me to accept,
And so I need Your celebration.

Thank You for Your presence, Father.
Amen.

Day 20

Ecclesiastes 7:23–29

23 All this I tested by wisdom and I said,

"I am determined to be wise"—
   but this was beyond me.
24 Whatever exists is far off and most profound—
   who can discover it?
25 So I turned my mind to understand,
      to investigate and to search out wisdom and the scheme
         of things
and to understand the stupidity of wickedness
      and the madness of folly.

26 I find more bitter than death
      the woman who is a snare,
   whose heart is a trap
      and whose hands are chains.
The man who pleases God will escape her,
      but the sinner she will ensnare.

27 "Look," says the Teacher, "this is what I have discovered:

"Adding one thing to another to discover the scheme of
         things—
      28 while I was still searching
      but not finding—
   I found one upright man among a thousand,
         but not one upright woman among them all.
         29 This only have I found:
            God created mankind upright,
               but they have gone in search of
                  many schemes."

From Schemers to Seekers

Arthur Jackson

God created mankind upright, but they have gone
in search of many schemes.

Ecclesiastes 7:29

*S*obered. That one word described how I felt as I casually perused the newspaper that arrived at my home. A retired law enforcement officer—indicted for his alleged crimes of sexual assault and kidnapping. A well-known celebrity—convicted of child pornography and enticing underage girls for sex. Crimes like these cause us to pause and ponder and mourn. But we also have to admit that even the more benign schemes of those who aren't criminals affirm the result of Solomon's search in Ecclesiastes 7:29. Eugene Peterson's *The Message* paraphrases this verse as "God made men and women true and upright, *we're* the ones who've made a mess of things."

A verse like this, and its context, holds up a mirror that we'd rather not peer into. We see this also in the apostle Paul's conclusion in Romans 3:23: "All have sinned and fall short of the glory of God." Among the Teacher's many discoveries (Ecclesiastes 7:27) was that no one gets a pass (v. 28). Schemers all! Sooner or later in life we become aware that—in inordinate and often devious ways—we're subject to scheming for self-preservation, self-exaltation, self-satisfaction, or self-fulfillment.

The good news, however, is this: even though we've strayed from God's design as manifested in our sinful thoughts, words, and deeds, we also have an invitation to return to Him. The human race's malady is sin, but the remedy is a Savior, Jesus Christ. Schemers who become sincere seekers of their Maker will become finders through a relationship with Jesus.

> When you ponder the sinful patterns of the world and those of your own heart, what words describe your feelings? What prayers rise in your heart for yourself and others as you think about the bent of humankind "to make a mess of things"?

New Testament Revelation

The Teacher is someone with great internal conflict. It's easy for us to focus on the moments when the Teacher proclaims beloved theological truths like God's justice (3:17) and the ways God brings meaning into human lives (v. 13). But these truths failed to answer many of the Teacher's questions. Often, the Teacher lifts up an orthodox theological truth only to quickly counter it with what in life seems to contradict it. For example, while God promises to bring justice (3:17), the world is filled with injustice (3:16; 4:1; 5:8–10). The Teacher's greatest obstacle to lasting hope was death (9:10).

Believers today can relate entirely to the Teacher's experience of the contradictions between what we believe about God's character and what we experience in a broken world. But we know of a source of hope the Teacher did not: Christ, who has defeated death and forever proves God's love.

Prayer

Dear Father, I confess that too often I trust my own wisdom,
My intelligence,
My experience,
My gut,
More than I trust You, Creator of all things.

Open my eyes to see Your hand in the workings of my life,
To hear the whisper of Your Spirit,
And trust the leading of Your Son.

In wisdom may I cling to You and not to a solution of
my own making.

For the sake of Your Son, and by the power of Your Spirit,
Lead my steps today, Father.

Amen.

Where do you need healing in an area
of brokenness and struggle? Share your
situation with God, and listen for His
loving response to you.

Day 21

Ecclesiastes 8:1–8

¹ *Who is like the wise?*
  Who knows the explanation of things?
A person's wisdom brightens their face
  and changes its hard appearance.

² *Obey the king's command, I say, because you took an oath*
before God. ³ *Do not be in a hurry to leave the king's presence.*
Do not stand up for a bad cause, for he will do whatever he
pleases. ⁴ *Since a king's word is supreme, who can say to him,*
"What are you doing?"

⁵ *Whoever obeys his command will come to no harm,*
  and the wise heart will know the proper time and
    procedure.
⁶ *For there is a proper time and procedure for every matter,*
  though a person may be weighed down by misery.

⁷ *Since no one knows the future,*
  who can tell someone else what is to come?
⁸ *As no one has power over the wind to contain it,*
  so no one has power over the time of their death.
As no one is discharged in time of war,
  so wickedness will not release those who practice it.

Unknown Ahead

Lisa M. Samra

Since no one knows the future, who can tell
someone else what is to come?

Ecclesiastes 8:7

What would you like to know about your future?" This icebreaker question—designed to facilitate easy, light conversation—took a different turn with Jill's straightforward answer: "Nothing."

As I probed Jill's surprising response, my friend in her early thirties spoke about the deep suffering and loss she had already experienced: the death of three children as the result of a genetic disorder and an aggressive breast cancer diagnosis. It was suffering she continued to endure only through the daily empowering presence of the Spirit and a strong church community. Jill recognized that she would never have been able to face the future if she knew at the beginning all that would unfold.

The ability to know how specific details about our lives will unfold is intriguing because it holds the possibility of being able to control them. But the writer of Ecclesiastes reminds us that "no one knows the future" (Ecclesiastes 8:7). As humans, we're finite beings with limitations. But even if we knew the future, the passage reminds us that we can't change the outcome. This powerlessness is pictured with three things beyond our control—wind, death, and decisions of powerful people (v. 8).

The answer Jill expressed can be seen as a beautiful embodiment of Jesus's teaching on facing the kind of uncertainty highlighted in Ecclesiastes. Jesus's compassionate response is "do not worry about tomorrow" (Matthew 6:34). Instead, we can entrust each day to God, who both knows the future and has control over it as He leads us through all of life's journey.

> How do you handle uncertainty?

Future: Unknown

In our text, we see a major theme of the book: Our inability to know the future (Ecclesiastes 8:7). We see this same idea in 6:12: "Who can tell [us] what will happen . . . after [we're] gone?" and in 7:14: "No one can discover anything about their future." Gloomy thoughts. Yet we can find comfort in the fact that God is in charge. He knows (v. 14). We can trust Him for our future. For those who fear God, "it will go better" (8:12). He has our times in His hands. Therefore, we're called to "be happy" and "do good" (3:12; 7:14).

> Ask God for what you need to face
> current worries, fears, or unknowns
> in your life.

Prayer

Almighty God, who sets the course of nations and rulers,
Bless those who govern.
I confess I do not always harbor an attitude of obedience to those
You have set in authority above me,
Nor do I always pray that they would be filled with wisdom.

But today I ask, as You would have me,
That You would guide them,
Bring them into godliness,
Teach them Your laws of life,
And through them bless the world.

For the sake of Your Son I ask,
Amen.

Day 22

Ecclesiastes 8:9–17

⁹ *All this I saw, as I applied my mind to everything done under the sun. There is a time when a man lords it over others to his own hurt.* ¹⁰ *Then too, I saw the wicked buried—those who used to come and go from the holy place and receive praise in the city where they did this. This too is meaningless.*

¹¹ *When the sentence for a crime is not quickly carried out, people's hearts are filled with schemes to do wrong.* ¹² *Although a wicked person who commits a hundred crimes may live a long time, I know that it will go better with those who fear God, who are reverent before him.* ¹³ *Yet because the wicked do not fear God, it will not go well with them, and their days will not lengthen like a shadow.*

¹⁴ *There is something else meaningless that occurs on earth: the righteous who get what the wicked deserve, and the wicked who get what the righteous deserve. This too, I say, is meaningless.* ¹⁵ *So I commend the enjoyment of life, because there is nothing better for a person under the sun than to eat and drink and be glad. Then joy will accompany them in their toil all the days of the life God has given them under the sun.*

¹⁶ *When I applied my mind to know wisdom and to observe the labor that is done on earth—people getting no sleep day or night—* ¹⁷ *then I saw all that God has done. No one can comprehend what goes on under the sun. Despite all their efforts to search it out, no one can discover its meaning. Even if the wise claim they know, they cannot really comprehend it.*

A Distant Gaze

Marvin Williams

> There is something else meaningless that occurs on earth: the righteous who get what the wicked deserve, and the wicked who get what the righteous deserve. This too, I say, is meaningless.
>
> Ecclesiastes 8:14

While enduring rolling seas or riding a spinning amusement park attraction, we can feel fine one moment and in the next moment experience cold sweats, dizziness, fatigue, and an inability to focus—the dreaded effects of motion sickness, when your senses are receiving conflicting information.

Solomon might have experienced a sort of spiritual motion sickness. Wicked people were being honored in the same city in which they committed their crimes (Ecclesiastes 8:10), sentences for criminals weren't "quicky carried out" (v. 11), wicked people were living "a long time" (v. 12), and the wicked got "what the righteous deserve" while the righteous got "what the wicked deserve" (v. 14). These injustices must have been dizzying to him. Because God is righteous and just, Solomon expected God to punish the wicked and reward the righteous. But he saw the exact opposite. This disparity between righteousness and unrighteousness was enough to tempt good people to do evil.

How can we fight spiritual motion sickness? The same way we handle physical motion sickness—facing forward and having a distant gaze. In Psalm 73:17–26, the writer encouraged us to stop looking at the injustice and inequities and instead draw close to God, worship Him, and understand life from His perspective. It's there, in His presence, that we gain our spiritual strength, stability, and sight.

On what are you fixing your attention these days? How might gazing on God prevent you from experiencing spiritual motion sickness?

Justice and God's Judgment

Here the Teacher questions God's justice. Where is God when the wicked prosper, live long lives, or don't seem to pay for their crimes (8:11–12, 14)? Yet he also offers an answer: "It will go better with those who fear God, who are reverent before him. Yet because the wicked do not fear God, it will not go well with them" (vv. 12–13). When will this occur? Not always in this life, but always in the life to come—in eternity. There will be a judgment (3:15–17; 12:14). When we are discouraged by the evil in our world, the writer of Psalm 73 encourages us to draw close to God and enter into His presence: the place to find His hope, His strength, and His perspective on our circumstances.

word study

Done

[*na'asah*] (v. 17)

The Teacher approaches his conclusion: "All this I saw, as I applied my mind to everything done under the sun" (8:9). Still, he has not arrived at his ultimate conclusion. He has instead reached the point where he acknowledges his own limitations in the pursuit of wisdom. This emanates from his realization that he is observing "all that God has done" (v. 17). The word for *done* is *na'asah* (1:9, 13), and means "to make, do, or manufacture."

The related word describing God's *work* (v. 17) is *ma'aseh* and carries the connotation of what God has accomplished (see also 7:13; 11:5). An important concept in Ecclesiastes, God's work is lasting and authoritative—it will "endure forever" and includes His sovereignty over the cosmos. This stands in vivid contrast to our work (*'amal*), which is meaningless toil by comparison.

Day 23

Ecclesiastes 9:1–10

¹ *So I reflected on all this and concluded that the righteous and the wise and what they do are in God's hands, but no one knows whether love or hate awaits them.* ² *All share a common destiny—the righteous and the wicked, the good and the bad, the clean and the unclean, those who offer sacrifices and those who do not.*

> *As it is with the good,*
>> *so with the sinful;*
> *as it is with those who take oaths,*
>> *so with those who are afraid to take them.*

³ *This is the evil in everything that happens under the sun: The same destiny overtakes all. The hearts of people, moreover, are full of evil and there is madness in their hearts while they live, and afterward they join the dead.* ⁴ *Anyone who is among the living has hope—even a live dog is better off than a dead lion!*

> ⁵ *For the living know that they will die,*
>> *but the dead know nothing;*
> *they have no further reward,*
>> *and even their name is forgotten.*

⁶ *Their love, their hate*
   and their jealousy have long since vanished;
never again will they have a part
   in anything that happens under the sun.

⁷ *Go, eat your food with gladness, and drink your wine with a joyful heart, for God has already approved what you do.* ⁸ *Always be clothed in white, and always anoint your head with oil.* ⁹ *Enjoy life with your wife, whom you love, all the days of this meaningless life that God has given you under the sun—all your meaningless days. For this is your lot in life and in your toilsome labor under the sun.* ¹⁰ *Whatever your hand finds to do, do it with all your might, for in the realm of the dead, where you are going, there is neither working nor planning nor knowledge nor wisdom.*

God-Given Opportunities

Poh Fang Chia

Whatever your hand finds to do, do it
with all your might.
Ecclesiastes 9:10

I've always wanted to learn how to play the cello. But I've never found the time to enroll in a class. Or, perhaps more accurately, I haven't made the time for it. I had thought that in heaven I could probably master that instrument. In the meantime, I wanted to focus on using my time in the particular ways God has called me to serve Him now.

Life is short, and we often feel the pressure to make the most of our time on Earth before it slips away. But what does that really mean?

As the Teacher contemplated the meaning of life, he offered two recommendations. First, we're to live in the most meaningful way we can, which includes fully enjoying the good things God allows us to experience in life, such as food and drink (Ecclesiastes 9:7), clothing and cologne (v. 8 NLT), marriage (v. 9), and all of God's good gifts—which might include learning how to play the cello!

His second recommendation was diligent work (v. 10). Life is full of opportunities, and there is always more work to be done. We're to take advantage of the opportunities God gives us, seeking His wisdom on how to prioritize work and play in a way that uses our gifting to serve Him.

Life is a wonderful gift from the Lord. We honor Him when we take pleasure both in His daily blessings and in meaningful service.

> Are you inclined to prioritize work or play?

On Death

One of the realities of Scripture is what scholars call *progressive revelation*. This does not mean that the Bible moves from error to truth. Rather, it moves from incompleteness to completeness. This principle is of critical importance when examining the Old Testament view of death and the afterlife. Because ancient Israel had incomplete understanding of life after death, they sought to unravel difficult questions of injustice and unfairness through the law or principle of retribution—which taught that righteousness and wickedness received their just rewards in this life. Psalm 73, however, is a testimony of a person who is disillusioned by the fact that this principle clearly is not working. When we move into the New Testament, we are given more information about God's dealing with us *after death*. This information helps us process injustice in our world with the understanding that one day the God of justice will make all things right.

word studies

Hope [*bitahon*] (v. 4) │ **Lot** [*cheleq*] (v. 9)

The word *hope* (Hebrew, *bitahon*, 9:4) does not connote hope for the next life. Rather, it is a hope tied to life "under the sun" (v. 3). With such a view, it is unsurprising that the Teacher observes "the dead know nothing" and "have no further reward" (v. 5). Yet he also tells us to enjoy our "lot in life" (v. 9, Hebrew, *cheleq*). The Teacher acknowledges God but too often looks horizontally. We know from his conclusion in 12:14 ("God will bring every deed into judgment, including every hidden thing, whether it is good or evil") that he anticipates a future reckoning with God. But when his focus is earthbound, hope is ephemeral and fleeting.

> In what ways is God calling you to serve or enjoy life?

Prayer

My Father in heaven, I know that I am but dust,
And, when the days of my life have come to an end,
To dust I will return.

But I confess that I live as though I will not die,
As if death itself has gone away.

Teach me to count my days for the blessings that they are,
To love those around me well,
And to love You well,
With the time You've given me.

May the life of Your Spirit shine in me,
For the sake of Your Son who leads me,

Amen.

Day 24

Ecclesiastes 9:11–18

[11] *I have seen something else under the sun:*

The race is not to the swift
or the battle to the strong,
nor does food come to the wise
or wealth to the brilliant
or favor to the learned;
but time and chance happen to them all.

[12] *Moreover, no one knows when their hour will come:*

As fish are caught in a cruel net,
or birds are taken in a snare,
so people are trapped by evil times
that fall unexpectedly upon them.

[13] *I also saw under the sun this example of wisdom that greatly impressed me:* [14] *There was once a small city with only a few people in it. And a powerful king came against it, surrounded it and built huge siege works against it.* [15] *Now there lived in that city a man poor but wise, and he saved the city by his wisdom. But nobody remembered that poor man.* [16] *So I said, "Wisdom is better than strength." But the poor man's wisdom is despised, and his words are no longer heeded.*

[17] *The quiet words of the wise are more to be heeded*
than the shouts of a ruler of fools.
[18] *Wisdom is better than weapons of war,*
but one sinner destroys much good.

It's Not Over Till It's Over

Mart DeHaan

The race is not to the swift or the battle to the strong.

Ecclesiastes 9:11

The headline read, "Jockey Beats Horse Over Finish Line." The jockey beat the pack by twenty lengths and his horse by one length when he was catapulted out of the saddle and over the finish line. His horse, which had tripped, followed soon after. But the victory went to the second-place finisher named Slip Up. A race official said that the jockey "was so far in front that only a freak accident would stop him, . . . and that's what happened."

We've all experienced life's unexpected happenings. The Teacher of Ecclesiastes took note of them when he said, "The race is not to the swift or the battle to the strong" (9:11). He reflected on the fact that we are not the master of our destiny, as we so often think we are.

Life is filled with unpredictable experiences and events. They seem like stones dropped into the gears of human ingenuity. A strong, healthy young adult drops dead. A rising young athlete contracts a crippling disease. A person of affluence suddenly loses everything in a bad deal.

What can we learn from this? Not to trust our own strength, our own wisdom, or our own skill, but to depend on the Lord who alone knows the end from the beginning.

Life's race is not over till He says it's over.

> Where have you seen "time and chance" (v. 11) fracture the way something should be or should have been?

Wisdom in Ecclesiastes

As Wisdom Literature, Ecclesiastes offers a mixed bag of statements on the value of wisdom overall. In 1:18, the Teacher says, "For with much wisdom comes much sorrow; the more knowledge, the more grief" but in 8:1 he counters, "Who is like the wise? Who knows the explanation of things? A person's wisdom brightens their face and changes its hard appearance." Why such mixed signals? Because life lived "under the sun" (that is, according to the wisdom and values of this world) is destructive. But a life transformed by God's wisdom can impact their world for good.

> Identify an area of your life where you are being invited not to trust in your own strength, wisdom, or skill but in God's? Talk to God about it.

Prayer

I make plans, good Father, for my life each day.
And though I know I cannot bring those plans to life
without Your grace,
Still I plan.

Help me to see Your hand in every minute of my day,
To hear Your quiet voice guiding my steps,
And to trust that You will always lead me home.

Help me to mean it when I say,
If God wills it.

Teach me to make my plans Your plans,
And to lean on You in each of them.

Amen.

Day 25

Ecclesiastes 10:1–11

¹ *As dead flies give perfume a bad smell,*
  so a little folly outweighs wisdom and honor.
² *The heart of the wise inclines to the right,*
  but the heart of the fool to the left.
³ *Even as fools walk along the road,*
  they lack sense
  and show everyone how stupid they are.
⁴ *If a ruler's anger rises against you,*
  do not leave your post;
  calmness can lay great offenses to rest.

⁵ *There is an evil I have seen under the sun,*
  the sort of error that arises from a ruler:
⁶ *Fools are put in many high positions,*
  while the rich occupy the low ones.
⁷ *I have seen slaves on horseback,*
  while princes go on foot like slaves.

⁸ *Whoever digs a pit may fall into it;*
  whoever breaks through a wall may be bitten by a snake.
⁹ *Whoever quarries stones may be injured by them;*
  whoever splits logs may be endangered by them.

¹⁰ *If the ax is dull*
  and its edge unsharpened,
more strength is needed,
  but skill will bring success.

¹¹ *If a snake bites before it is charmed,*
  the charmer receives no fee.

A Little Folly

Dave Branon

A little folly outweighs wisdom and honor.
Ecclesiastes 10:1

The British constable claims it was a mistake. However, the people in charge of his law enforcement career didn't see it that way. They said he scanned a bag of carrots and paid seven pence for them, but he also walked out of the store with a box of unpurchased donuts that should have cost him nearly ten pounds. As a result, the man with an otherwise perfect record as an officer lost his job. Even worse, he lost his good reputation.

The reality of this sad situation points to a truth Solomon detailed in Ecclesiastes 10. He says that "a little folly outweighs wisdom and honor" (v. 1). Putting it in terms we can smell, Solomon said folly is like having a dead fly in a container of perfume. It cancels out the beauty of the perfume and gives off a bad odor.

Solomon goes deeper into the consequences of foolishness: One who makes unwise decisions "lack[s] sense" (v. 3), and a person who digs a pit "may fall into it" (v. 8). But the wise? That person gravitates toward what is right (v. 2) and reacts with "calmness" to anger, which can "lay great offenses to rest" (v. 4).

No folly is little, after all, because it can lead to big consequences. Solomon's wise words, given through the Holy Spirit's inspiration, guide us as we seek to honor God by using wisdom to preserve our good reputation and persevere through life's challenges.

In Ecclesiastes 10:1, foolishness is compared to a stench. Where have you experienced the consequences of folly as being like a bad odor?

Folly versus Wisdom

In Ecclesiastes, wisdom and folly are often set in sharp contrast. Folly (or the fool) is tied to wickedness (7:17; 10:12) and is the opposite of wisdom (2:19). As Michael Eaton in his commentary on Ecclesiastes states, "[Folly] results from an inner deficiency of the personality (10:2) which becomes obvious to observers (v. 3), especially in the fool's speech (v. 14)."[13] In Jeremiah we read that the foolish are "skilled in doing evil" (4:22) and lack moral sensitivity: They're "senseless people, who have eyes but do not see, who have ears but do not hear" (5:21).

Identify whether there's an unwise path on which you're walking, and confess your ways to God.

When Life Isn't Fair

In chapter 10, we find proverbs like those in the book of Proverbs. What is a proverb? It's a general principle saying that wisdom leads to success. But here (see v. 6) and throughout the book, the author of Ecclesiastes invites us also to notice when general principles are upended. For example, sometimes—no matter how hard we try—our work backfires (2:21–22). (Or worse, wicked people are rewarded for evil actions—see 8:10, 14; 6:2.)

In an ordered, just universe, the law of cause and effect says that our actions influence outcomes. But exceptions exist. And so, the good, beautiful, and fair order of the universe breaks down—making life's meaning hard to grasp.

Day 26

Ecclesiastes 10:12–20

¹² Words from the mouth of the wise are gracious,
   but fools are consumed by their own lips.
¹³ At the beginning their words are folly;
   at the end they are wicked madness—
¹⁴ and fools multiply words.

No one knows what is coming—
   who can tell someone else what will happen after them?

¹⁵ The toil of fools wearies them;
   they do not know the way to town.

¹⁶ Woe to the land whose king was a servant
   and whose princes feast in the morning.
¹⁷ Blessed is the land whose king is of noble birth
   and whose princes eat at a proper time—
   for strength and not for drunkenness.

¹⁸ Through laziness, the rafters sag;
   because of idle hands, the house leaks.

¹⁹ A feast is made for laughter,
   wine makes life merry,
   and money is the answer for everything.

²⁰ Do not revile the king even in your thoughts,
   or curse the rich in your bedroom,
   because a bird in the sky may carry your words,
   and a bird on the wing may report what
   you say.

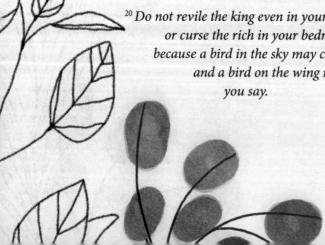

Words of the Wise

Cindy Hess Kasper

Words from the mouth of the wise are gracious.

Ecclesiastes 10:12

My niece's husband recently posted on social media: "I would say a lot more online if it weren't for this little voice that prompts me not to. As a follower of Jesus, you might think that little voice is the Holy Spirit. It isn't. It's my wife, Heidi."

With the smile comes a sobering thought. The cautions of a discerning friend can reflect the wisdom of God. Ecclesiastes 10 says that the "words from the mouth of the wise are gracious" (v. 12); and in chapter 9, "Words of the wise, spoken quietly, should be heard (v. 17 NKJV).

Scripture warns us not to be wise in our own eyes or proud (Proverbs 3:7; Isaiah 5:21; Romans 12:16). In other words, let's not assume that we have all the answers! James 1:19 says, "Everyone should be quick to listen, slow to speak." God can use others—whether it is a friend, a spouse, a pastor, or a coworker—to teach us more of His wisdom.

"Wisdom reposes in the heart of the discerning," declares the book of Proverbs (14:33). Part of recognizing the Spirit's wisdom is discovering how to listen and learn from each other.

> Identify someone who has given
> you wise counsel.

> Discern how you are being invited
> to listen to someone's wisdom in this season.

Finally: It's Time to Build!

Now that the Teacher has spent much of the book demolishing our optimism in our own capabilities, the site is leveled for rebuilding. Without allowing us to forget that we live in a broken, unjust world, the Teacher increasingly offers scaffolding for living well, including: Have integrity and wisdom (10:5–19). Take risks (11:1–6). Live wholeheartedly and joyfully (vv. 9–10). Even though living with wisdom, boldness, and joy will not prevent our death or guarantee our success, the Teacher advises these are better options than the alternatives. Ultimately, these actions characterize a God-centered life—which is the culminating wisdom of the book—the foundation on which the author's message rests (12:1, 13).

Prayer

Father, I confess I am often too quick to speak,
And too slow to listen.

Teach me to restrain my mouth when wisdom would have
me be silent.

Help me this day to use my words to bless,
To bring kindness into the lives of others,
To proclaim the goodness of your grace,
And to uphold the blessings of peace.

Fill my mouth with the words Your Son would say,
By the power of the Spirit,
For your glory, dear Father.

Amen.

Day 27

Ecclesiastes 11:1–6

[1] *Ship your grain across the sea;*
   after many days you may receive a return.
[2] *Invest in seven ventures, yes, in eight;*
   you do not know what disaster may come upon the land.

[3] *If clouds are full of water,*
   they pour rain on the earth.
Whether a tree falls to the south or to the north,
   in the place where it falls, there it will lie.
[4] *Whoever watches the wind will not plant;*
   whoever looks at the clouds will not reap.

[5] *As you do not know the path of the wind,*
   or how the body is formed in a mother's womb,
so you cannot understand the work of God,
   the Maker of all things.

[6] *Sow your seed in the morning,*
   and at evening let your hands not be idle,
for you do not know which will succeed,
   whether this or that,
   or whether both will do equally well.

Now's the Time

Alyson Kieda

Sow your seed in the morning, and at evening let
your hands not be idle.

Ecclesiastes 11:6

I enjoy my two small vegetable plots, but they take lots of work. In May, I turned over the soil, added fertilizer, and then planted and watered the seedlings (which I started inside in early spring). That was just the beginning. Every day that it didn't rain, I needed to water the gardens—sometimes twice—and keep the weeds pulled. Diligence was required!

My husband and I once came home from a week away and discovered both plots were overflowing with weeds. A friend had watered the garden, but I hadn't asked her to pull weeds. (That would be taxing our friendship!) It took me hours to pull out all the nasty things.

In Ecclesiastes 11, the author talks about the importance of diligence. Instead of waiting for the perfect time to plant, for example, farmers needed to move forward. If they waited, neither sowing nor reaping occurred (v. 4). They were to "sow [their] seed in the morning, and at evening let [their] hands not be idle" (v. 6).

No matter our work, attentiveness and conscientiousness are required. The apostle Paul wrote, "Whatever you do, work at it with all your heart, as working for the Lord" (Colossians 3:23). But we can trust the results to God. He makes what we do grow (1 Corinthians 3:7–9). When we work diligently for Him, He ensures we reap the fruit of our labor—now and for eternity (Colossians 3:24).

Identify a task or responsibility God has entrusted to you in this season. How might you "work at it with all your heart, as working for the Lord" (Colossians 3:23)? Commit your task to God, listening for His heart toward you.

About: Themes

In the Teacher's final chapters, he continues themes he wrangled over in previous chapters: taking risks and making wise choices (11:1–6), enjoying life (11:7–10), and remembering (fearing, obeying, and following) God while still young (12:1–8). If the author is King Solomon, we know he enjoyed many pleasures. God blessed him with wisdom and untold wealth, so he could buy the best of everything (2 Chronicles 1:10–12). He had a harem of seven hundred wives from other nations and three hundred concubines (women of lower status than a wife). He disobeyed God's command to the Israelites: "You must not intermarry with them, because they will surely turn your hearts after their gods" (1 Kings 11:2), which they did (v. 3).

It's fitting that he concludes with the theme of remembering God: "Fear God and keep his commandments" (Ecclesiastes 12:13). Doing so helps promote wise decisions and true enjoyment of life.

The Gift of Work

Scripture describes human beings as those created in the image of a creative, working God (Exodus 20:11; Genesis 2:1–2) and given work as a gift (v. 15). Humanity was called to "fill the earth and subdue it" (1:28)—entrusted with caring for creation and developing creation's potential. After humanity's fall into sin, however, Scripture says work will become difficult and frustrating (3:17–19).

The Teacher in Ecclesiastes captures both work's joy and its frustration. The fulfillment we find in work is described as one of life's greatest joys (Ecclesiastes 5:19–20). A person absorbed by satisfying work isn't focused on or tormented by life's unanswerable questions (v. 20). But envy (4:4), isolation (v. 8), and the inability to ensure the future impact of our work (2:19–23) can taint work's joy. And the Teacher warned that the human appetite for more is difficult to satisfy, even with work (6:7).

Day 28

Ecclesiastes 11:7–10

⁷ *Light is sweet,*
and it pleases the eyes to see the sun.
⁸ *However many years anyone may live,*
let them enjoy them all.
But let them remember the days of darkness,
for there will be many.
Everything to come is meaningless.

⁹ *You who are young, be happy while you are young,*
and let your heart give you joy in the days of your youth.
Follow the ways of your heart
and whatever your eyes see,
but know that for all these things
God will bring you into judgment.
¹⁰ *So then, banish anxiety from your heart*
and cast off the troubles of your body,
for youth and vigor are meaningless.

Follow His Heart

Linda Washington

Follow the ways of your heart . . . but know that
for all these things God will bring you
into judgment.

Ecclesiastes 11:9

Y ou've got to find what you love," Steve Jobs said to graduates in a standout Stanford University commencement address in 2005. The advice he gave, that of "following your heart," is a common theme for the best commencement speeches of all time. Other topics he mentioned that frequently appear in graduation speeches are "discover your purpose" and "be prepared to fail."

King Solomon also had advice about following one's heart in Ecclesiastes 11:7–10 to help young people avoid a life filled with regret. Verse 9 says, "You who are young, be happy while you are young, and let your heart give you joy in the days of your youth. Follow the ways of your heart and whatever your eyes see." If we're honest, we want the advice to end there. But he continues: "But know that for all these things God will bring you into judgment." In other words, there can be a cost for choosing to follow one's heart if we leave God out of the picture.

Life is not all about us following *our* plans. If we trust Jesus as Savior, He has a stake in what we do. We exist to bring glory to Him. Psalm 115:1 says, "Not to us, LORD, not to us but to your name be the glory." Though we may gain wisdom as we mature, we will never "graduate" toward complete independence. We will always need God. Only He can help us discover our purpose—to follow *His* heart—and succeed even after a failure.

> How are your goals a reflection of God's?
> What are the ways you've shown others
> His heart of compassion this week?

Do I Matter?

One of the big questions Ecclesiastes has us ask ourselves is this—do I matter? In the opening, the Teacher concludes we don't. We're just another blip in life's inexorable cycle: "Generations come and generations go. . . . No one remembers [us]" (1:4, 11). From "under the sun" (v. 3), our very limited viewpoint, we are insignificant. But above the sun—and to a God who sees the big picture—there is a different story. Here and in the conclusion, the author says God sees our actions and cares about the details of our lives (11:9; 12:14). That is, our actions extend beyond the temporal into eternity. So, do we matter? Because we matter to God, the author's final word is a resounding yes.

Prayer

Thank You, Father, for Your gifts to me.

*The fingerprints of Your design are on my passions, my intellect, the
work of my hands.*

*Open my eyes to see what You would have me do with this life,
These talents,
This time,
So the world will know that I am Yours.*

*Awaken in me the power of Your Spirit to bring beauty from darkness,
Hope from sadness,
And love from barren hearts.*

*Make me a light for the glory of Your Son,
By the power of Your Spirit,
For Your reputation alone, my great Father.*

Amen.

Day 29

Ecclesiastes 12:1–8

[1] *Remember your Creator*
    in the days of your youth,
before the days of trouble come
    and the years approach when you will say,
    "I find no pleasure in them"—
[2] *before the sun and the light*
    and the moon and the stars grow dark,
    and the clouds return after the rain;
[3] *when the keepers of the house tremble,*
    and the strong men stoop,
when the grinders cease because they are few,
    and those looking through the windows grow dim;
[4] *when the doors to the street are closed*
    and the sound of grinding fades;
when people rise up at the sound of birds,
    but all their songs grow faint;
[5] *when people are afraid of heights*
    and of dangers in the streets;
when the almond tree blossoms
    and the grasshopper drags itself along
    and desire no longer is stirred.
Then people go to their eternal home
    and mourners go about the streets.

⁶ Remember him—before the silver cord is severed,
* and the golden bowl is broken;*
before the pitcher is shattered at the spring,
* and the wheel broken at the well,*
⁷ and the dust returns to the ground it came from,
* and the spirit returns to God who gave it.*

⁸ "Meaningless! Meaningless!" says the Teacher.
* "Everything is meaningless!"*

Life's Greatest Treasure

James Banks

Remember your Creator . . .
Ecclesiastes 12:1

I'd love to find some sea glass." It was a simple prayer as I walked along a sparse beach one hot summer day. I had gone some distance and found nothing but kept looking. Three miles later a young, attractive woman walked toward me. I smiled at her and then looked away, recalling God's advice to be careful "with my eyes" (Job 31:1). The moment I diverted my glance I saw it. Two steps away was a beautifully weathered piece of sea glass. If I hadn't turned my head, I would have missed it. Did God reward my thinking of Him? Hard to say, but I was glad I did.

Books such as Job, Proverbs, and Ecclesiastes are referred to as "Wisdom Literature" because they help us discover the blessings and wisdom of walking with God and the meaninglessness of life apart from Him. "Remember your Creator in the days of your youth, before the days of trouble come," Ecclesiastes 12:1 reminds us. The writer (Solomon) goes on to poetically but graphically describe our bodies' decline as we age: our legs ("the strong men") become weaker, teeth fail ("the grinders cease"), eyesight lessens ("the windows grow dim"; v. 3).

Solomon's point isn't to be morbid about aging but rather to divert our gaze to our ultimate purpose in all of life. God made us and loves us, and as we turn our hearts to Him, we discover the greatest treasure of all.

> What practical steps will you take to turn to God today? How is He your greatest treasure?

About: Poem

Ecclesiastes 12:1–7 is a metaphorical poem that mirrors the poem in chapter one. Both touch on life's fleeting nature and fragility. Here, the "days of trouble" (v. 1) refer to the difficulties of one's older years when one loses pleasure in what once brought joy. In verse 3, we see the deterioration of the body's strength, loss of teeth ("grinders"), and dulling of eyesight. The aged awake early "at the sound of birds" (v. 4), yet the birds' songs are faint due to a loss of hearing. In verse 5, fears increase because of fragile bodies. But verses 6–7 add hope: We're to "remember him [God]" now before it's too late. Believers have the hope of renewed bodies and eternal life (2 Corinthians 5:1).

word study

Remember

[*zakhar*] (v. 1)

In the Old Testament, remembrance is more than memorizing trivia. Remembering "usually leads to action."[14] To "remember God" is to reflect on God's faithfulness and, out of that knowledge, be moved to surrender to God's ways. Its opposite? Arrogantly trusting in ourselves. For example, Deuteronomy 8:11–20 warns of the dangers of forgetting God: "Do not say to yourself, 'My power and the might of my own hand have gotten me this wealth.' But remember [*zakhar*] the LORD your God, for it is he who gives you power to get wealth" (vv. 17–18 NRSV).

The call to "remember God" (12:1) is a key turning point in Ecclesiastes. Throughout Ecclesiastes, the Teacher exposes the folly of forgetting God by showing us our limitations. Through remembering God (Ecclesiastes 12:1), we unlock the door to a gratitude-filled, God-centered life.

Day 30

Ecclesiastes 12:9–14

⁹ Not only was the Teacher wise, but he also imparted knowledge to the people. He pondered and searched out and set in order many proverbs. ¹⁰ The Teacher searched to find just the right words, and what he wrote was upright and true.

¹¹ The words of the wise are like goads, their collected sayings like firmly embedded nails—given by one shepherd. ¹² Be warned, my son, of anything in addition to them.

Of making many books there is no end, and much study wearies the body.

¹³ Now all has been heard;
  here is the conclusion of the matter:
Fear God and keep his commandments,
  for this is the duty of all mankind.
¹⁴ For God will bring every deed into judgment,
  including every hidden thing,
  whether it is good or evil.

A Beautiful Epitaph

Lisa M. Samra

Here is the conclusion of the matter: Fear God
and keep his commandments.

Ecclesiastes 12:13

From famous burial grounds to small graveyards, I'm drawn to cemeteries and the stories they hold. I've unexpectedly smiled at the remembrances etched in stone. I've shed tears over brief inscriptions that tell the story of a life. One headstone I've not forgotten has four names inscribed alongside their mother's; the dates convey the unbearable truth that each child's life ended before their first birthday.

After all the ways the writer of Ecclesiastes has explored life's fleeting nature, we might anticipate a lengthy summary to close the book. Instead, like a brief epitaph on a gravestone, the short, meaningful conclusion is to "fear God and keep his commandments" (Ecclesiastes 12:13).

To fear God is to have a right relationship with Him, to recognize that God is the Creator and Ruler over all creation, and we're not. We release the stress of trying to control our lives and instead entrust ourselves to Him.

Embracing the wisdom of Ecclesiastes directs us to follow the greatest commandment given by Jesus: "Love the Lord your God with all your heart and with all your soul and with all your mind" (Matthew 22:37). This wholehearted devotion provides joy instead of anxiety.

When this life's journey ends, the truths that spring from the book of Ecclesiastes and find fulfillment in Jesus can produce a beautiful epitaph of our lives—that with all our heart, soul, and mind, we loved God.

> Did anything from this study
> surprise you?

Closing Thoughts

Chapter 12 began with the instruction to remember our Creator. This goes beyond mere acknowledgment. We have an obligation. "Fear God and obey his commandments," says the Teacher (12:13). Jesus said, "If you love me, keep my commands" (John 14:15). What commandments? "Love the Lord your God with all your heart and with all your soul and with all your mind," and "love your neighbor as yourself" (Matthew 22:37–39; also see John 15:12). Jesus added, "Anyone who loves me will obey my teaching. My Father will love them, and we will come to them and make our home with them" (John 14:23).

Everything Made New

While our journey began with "everything is meaningless [*hebel*]," *hebel* is not where we end. In the conclusion, the author directs our eyes above the sun, inviting us to worship the One who holds everything—life's uncertainties, our future, and the universe—in His hands (12:13). The Teacher encourages us that through living in trusting dependence on God, we are free to enjoy God and His good gifts (12:13; 11:9).

We read in Romans 8:20–21, "The creation was subjected to frustration . . . in hope that the creation itself will be liberated from its bondage." In the biblical Greek, "frustration" in verse 20 is the same word for *hebel* in Ecclesiastes of the Greek Old Testament. According to Romans, one day, *hebel* will be defeated—the curse of sin's binding will break. Everything will be made new (Revelation 21:1–4). *Hebel* will not have the last word.[15]

> As you finish your time in Ecclesiastes, identify a truth from the book that you wish to keep in your mind and heart.

Notes

1. Jim Winter, *Opening Up Ecclesiastes* (Leominster, England: Day One Publications, 2005).

2. David A. Dorsey, *The Literary Structure of the Old Testament: A Commentary on Genesis–Malachi* (Grand Rapids, MI: Baker Academic, 1999), 194, 197–98.

3. David A. Dorsey, *The Literary Structure of the Old Testament: A Commentary on Genesis–Malachi* (Grand Rapids, MI: Baker Academic, 1999), 197.

4. Derek Kidner, *The Message of Ecclesiastes: A Time to Mourn and a Time to Dance* (Downers Grove, IL: InterVarsity, 1976), 87.

5. Adapted from David A. Dorsey, *The Literary Structure of the Old Testament: A Commentary on Genesis–Malachi* (Grand Rapids, MI: Baker Academic, 1999), 198. If you're interested in learning more about the structure, context, and meaning of Ecclesiastes, check out the recommended reading list on page 141.

6. David A. Dorsey, *The Literary Structure of the Old Testament: A Commentary on Genesis–Malachi* (Grand Rapids, MI: Baker Academic, 1999), 193–94.

7. Edward M. Curtis, *Ecclesiastes and Song of Songs*, Teach the Text Commentary Series, ed. Mark L. Strauss and John H. Walton (Grand Rapids, MI: Baker, 2013), 27.

8. Derek Kidner, *The Message of Ecclesiastes: A Time to Mourn and a Time to Dance* (Downers Grove, IL: InterVarsity, 1976), 107.

9. Warren W. Wiersbe, *Be Satisfied: Looking for the Answer to the Meaning of Life* (Wheaton, IL: Victor Books, 1990), 82.

10. Derek Kidner, *The Message of Ecclesiastes: A Time to Mourn and a Time to Dance* (Downers Grove, IL: InterVarsity, 1976), 87.

11. David A. Dorsey, *The Literary Structure of the Old Testament: A Commentary on Genesis–Malachi* (Grand Rapids, MI: Baker Academic, 1999), 195.

12. David A. Dorsey, *The Literary Structure of the Old Testament: A Commentary on Genesis–Malachi* (Grand Rapids, MI: Baker Academic, 1999), 193–94.

13. Michael A. Eaton, *Ecclesiastes: An Introduction and Commentary* (Downers Grove, IL: InterVarsity, 1983), 133.

14. Matthew Richard Schlimm, *70 Hebrew Words Every Christian Should Know* (Nashville: Abingdon, 2018), 98.

15. Edward M. Curtis, *Ecclesiastes and Song of Songs,* Teach the Text Commentary Series, ed. Mark L. Strauss and John H. Walton (Grand Rapids , MI: Baker, 2013), 109.

Resources for Further Study on Ecclesiastes

- Bartholomew, Craig G. *Ecclesiastes*. Baker Commentary on the Old Testament Wisdom and Psalms. Edited by Tremper Longman III. Grand Rapids, MI: Baker Academic, 2009.

- Curtis, Edward M. *Ecclesiastes and Song of Songs*. Teach the Text Commentary Series. Edited by Mark L. Strauss and John H. Walton. Grand Rapids, MI: Baker, 2013.

- Dorsey, David A. "Ecclesiastes." In *The Literary Structure of the Old Testament: A Commentary on Genesis–Malachi*. Grand Rapids, MI: Baker Academic, 1999.

- Kidner, Derek. *The Message of Ecclesiastes: A Time to Mourn and a Time to Dance*. The Bible Speaks Today Series. Edited by J. A. Motyer. Downers Grove, IL: InterVarsity, 1984.